INDEX

Chapter	Page	
1	1	The Beginning.
2	6	Harry and Edna my father and mother.
3	32	Family breakdown.
4	38	Training 15 to 18 years old.
5	41	Years 18 and beyond—Army life.
6	47	Life after playing. The Hadfield F.C. Foundation.
7	57	Employment.
8	64	Sport.
9	69	The Forster Cup and Saucer Tournaments.
10	73	Volunteering.
11	75	Reunions.
12	86	Weddings in my Family.
13	90	A bit about Forster.
14	92	Travel and Holidays.
15	99	Eightieth Birthday Parties.
16	102	The Guildford Farm.
17	112	The Hadfield F.C. Ball and Disaster.
18	120	Conclusion.
19	125	Addendums and Postscript.

THE FOX CLAN and MY STORY,

WARTS and ALL.

Author Neville Fox   Chapter 1

THE BEGINNING.

The Fox Clan can be traced back to Robert Fox in the late 1600s. It is known that he was the father of 6 children the third being Roger born 1737. Roger & Hannah were also to parent 6 children the third being Thomas born 1768. Thomas and his wife Elizabeth Coates had three children, their first being John born November 1789. In 1817 John married Elizabeth Clarkson, somewhat in haste, their first child William was born 6 months later. They were to produce 13 children.

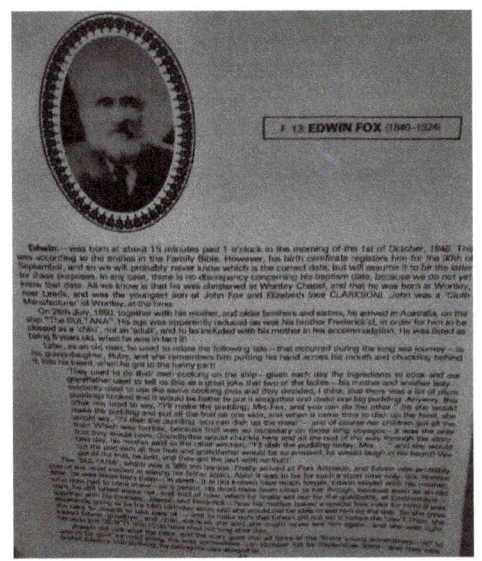

My Great Grand Father Edwin

I take up the story in some detail from here on as this story is my contribution to the preservation of the Fox Clan to my following kin. I am in my eighties and with my demise who is left to tell some of the history, some of the hardships and some of the stories of the past.

Going back to John and Elizabeth for a moment. It is told that John was a woollen cloth manufacturer. He had a successful mill in Leeds, County of York, England, where a woollen serge was manufactured which was used in the making of uniforms for the forces and suits for English gentlemen. It is told but can be argued that the serge was known as Fox's Serge. Every Fox in that trade at the time was only too eager to claim that recognition.

Somewhere between 1840 and 1848 it is understood that John backed a bill for an Englishman who later defaulted. John became responsible for the debt causing his business to fail. A significant rethink of the family future was imminent. The decision was to migrate to Australia.

John boarded the "Belle Alliance" or the "Calcutta" saying goodbye to Leeds, County of York, his country England, his friends and most soul destroying, his wife Elizabeth and his twelve living children. One had died in infancy. John was to do it alone until he had re-established himself in the woollen industry. He became a tailor and draper in Bowden South Australia.

Within about 12 months of his arrival, he had established himself. With money in his pocket, it was time to send for Elizabeth and family. For reasons I am not aware of Elizabeth and seven children left England on the long journey to Adelaide Australia arriving on 26.7.1850. The youngest to make the trip was, nine years old Edwin, my great grandfather.

Whilst the family was on route to Australia on the Sultana, John became very ill. In those days his illness was called "inflammation of the bowels". Today it is called bowel cancer. On docking at Adelaide John was not there to meet them.

It is told that Elizabeth owed 23 pounds to cover all or part of the fares. They would have been frantic, not knowing anyone, dumped on the wharf in unfamiliar circumstances and wondering where they were going to stay. John eventually struggled from his sick bed and belatedly met them at the port and I suppose paid the 23 pounds.

John's illness gradually took its toll on him, and he passed away on 27.2.1851, approximately 6 months after the family's arrival. The family were once again on their own. He was buried at Hindmarsh Cemetery on 2.3.1851. A tragic end to a family that were looking forward to better days.

Following John's death Elizabeth decided to take her family to Horsham, Victoria. It is not fully known why Horsham was the selected destination. One theory is that she went with her recently married daughter Christiana whom, it is thought had her husband's relatives there. Some 2 or 3 years later three of the boys decided the gold fields in and around Castlemaine, Victoria was the place to make their millions.

Joseph, Frederick and Edwin yoked up their horses and drays and set off to the gold fields. They thought that using their horses and drays carting tailings and dirt to be washed was to be their avenue to riches. On the way Edwin had his fourteenth birthday. His mother had made him a birthday cake putting it in the care of Joseph to be opened and eaten on his birthday and not a day earlier. On arrival at the gold fields, it didn't take them long to get to work satisfying the miners with their horses and drays. They worked hard and saved hard as their ambitions were to buy land and start farming. Joseph, the eldest purchased his first farm at Campbells Creek, near Castlemaine prior to his marriage to Mary Ann Hooper in 1854. Edwin, my great grandfather, the youngest of the family purchased his farm at Strathloddon, near Yapeen and Castlemaine when he was 21. He spent about 7 years in the gold fields earning enough money to commence his passion, FARMING.

Edwin married Mary Wells in August 1862 and together they had 12 children. Mary was born in Launceston Tasmania on 27.6.1844. Her family shifted to the mainland settling in Vaughan again near Castlemaine and the gold fields. Her father, Frederick Richard Wells was a miner. As Vaughan was in the middle of the gold fields this seemed a sound choice for more than one reason. Strathloddon and Vaughan are adjacent hamlets whilst Frederick Wells was close to his work it was also close to Edwin's farm where naturally, Mary and Edwin met resulting in their marriage and the births of their 12 children.

Edwin was mainly into sheep and the wool industry. When the gold got less and less the miners and others left the Castlemaine and Guildford districts. He had done well up to now and bought more properties. It is accepted that he purchased four farms in and around his Strathloddon property. It is understood that the properties were, Woods, Laundys, Kelly's and Carters.

Edwin's main home was in Yapeen. There was also a small cottage on Kelly's in Guildford. It was in this cottage that Edwin's second son John, born 11.4.1870 and his wife Jane, nee Atkinson born 3.7.1867, lived for some years rearing 8 children. Their second son or third child Harry Atkinson Fox, my father, showed a keen interest in animals and farming. He was often helping his father John and grandfather Edwin learning all he could about farming.

When Harry was 9 ½ years old, Kelly's cottage burned down. John, Jane and their 8 children shifted into Edwin's house in Yapeen. Edwin and wife Mary built a smaller home in Yapeen pending their retirement. They named their new home "Leeds Cottage". I suppose this was a reminder from where he came from in England all those years ago.

Edwin and son John became partners growing copious amounts of oaten hay to feed the many horses in the district. Every farmer had teams for farm work, probably a cart or sulky light horse and a hack for riding. They would transport their produce by wagon to the merchants and marketplaces in the area. This resulted in a comfortable living.

My father Harry became his father's righthand man. John found other work by contracting in road forming and spent a lot of time away from home, camping on site. It is assumed Harry took to this lifestyle as we will read about later. In 1916 John and Jane moved their address to Guildford to what is now known as "Fox's Hill" situated on the Vaughan/Tarilta Road. Later in my story it will be talked about a lot more as Harry, my father, later purchased it from his family and so did I after Harry's passing.

EARLY EDUCATION

Up to 1877 education was by private schooling costing Edwin one shilling (10 cents} per child per week. A small fortune for Edwin and Mary to have their 12 children educated. A government school was established in Strathloddon on 1.6.1877. Hopefully the government schooling system went some of the way relieving Edwin of the one shilling a week per child expense.

The school number was 1903 and the headmaster was Mr Mark A Pitt. John attended the school opening on the first day, he was given number 7 on the school's public registers. In 1904 there was a renaming of the Strathloddon school to Yapeen. John's children including my father attended Yapeen school.

A booklet by Raymond A Bradfield titled "A Century of Schooldays 1877 - 1977" possibly available from National Library of Australia Card Number and ISBN   0 9599153 4 6 brings a lot of Yapeen school and district history with photos and script.

FINDING EDWIN. The Foxes from Edwin through to Harry (and my sister Margaret Priest) are all buried in the Campbells Creek Cemetery on the back hill, all except Edwin. Edwin's grave hadn't been found in many years. On visiting the family plot in 2018, a grave digger told me that there was another Fox buried down nearer the front gate and about 20 meters in from a large pine tree. I fossicked through all the deteriorated head stones and found Edwin's and Mary's with Fox being the only word barely recognisable. I got the head stone restored as my contribution to the Clan and so future visitors to the cemetery might be able to locate it.

Area searched   *original head stone*   *Restored head stone*

It was quite weird how I was able to find someone to refurbish and re-paint the lettering. I rang the Cemetery Trust, at the time it was manned by a woman volunteer. I asked her if there was someone that could restore the head stone. She said, "As a matter of fact there is a gentleman standing next to me that can put you right. " Sure enough a chap from Harcourt came on the phone. "Send me $100 for a paint job or $500 for gold lettering", he said. I sent him his $100 and the lettering job was done in black. I have seen the finished job and it's very good. See the results above for yourself.

Chapter 2

HARRY and EDNA, my father and mother

To advance the story of the Fox clan we must dwell for a while on Harry and Edna. John and Jane's third child Harry was born on 18.6.1899.

Harry Atkinson Fox

Born Tarilta 18/6/1899

Died 26/9/1985 age 86

Edna Albania Hicks

Born Corop 11/5/1906.

Died 13/10/1982 age 76.

Edna Hicks was born on 11.5.1906. They were married on 27.6.1928. Edna was born and bred in Corop, a small village near Rochester in central Victoria. She schooled in Corop and worked in the family store and Post Office owned by her father and mother, James, and Albania Hicks. At this stage Harry was contracting on the irrigation channel system in or near Corop and become interested in the young lady working in the store. Incidentally the irrigation system feeds water from the Waranga Basin reservoir situated between Rushworth, Murchison and Tatura to the Mallee via the Mallee channel and its subsidiaries. This water system has made a parched and desolate area of Victoria into a rich food bowl.

Sparks must have flown between the two as they were duly married in 1928. In the days of their courtship Edna taught Sunday school and played the organ at the Corop Methodist church. It has been told on many occasions that Harry, wanting to impress, rode a cow complete with bell round and round the church. The louder the bell rang and clanged the louder Edna thumped the pedals and keys on the organ. Harry was always a prankster.

THE LAKE CARGELLIGO ENCOUNTER.

Shortly after their marriage Harry had the urge to get back to farming which his father John and grandfather Edwin had nurtured him in.

He and Edna acquired a 1000-acre block near Lake Cargelligo. NSW. Harry's uncle Thomas Henry Atkinson known as Howie or Ackie, which is short for Atkinson, also acquired a similar parcel of land either adjacent or quite nearby. This land was a government initiative to open up and develop the land for pasture and/or cropping. The government gave the land for free for a number of years before payments were required. It was an incentive to work long and hard to clear scrub and trees in readiness for the planting of pasture or crop. In conjunction with these activities a home had to be built. Keep in mind that we are talking about the early 1900s, machinery and tools were primitive. This was pioneering at its best. Bloody hard and relentless work.

THEIR FIRST HOME.

Edna told a story to her mother about her first house. Her mother wrote to her asking about her house. Edna's answer was "Everything is fine, I have carpets to match the walls. Don't worry". Her mother was satisfied with her reply. The truth was she had a tent and bag humpy with bags on the ground. Hence carpet to match the walls. Her organ that she played at the Corop church was stored under a multitude of bags to keep it dry. Sometime later a proper house was built. That house still stands today with some modifications. I had the privilege to visit it with my eldest sister Doris some years ago. More of that will be talked further into my story.

It is believed that Harry "went on the road" searching for work with his 16-horse team doing whatever to earn a few quid so the family could eat. There was no income from the farm until such time that crops were sown, harvested and sold at which stage part of the loan had to be paid. As stated, it was bloody hard.

HARRY'S STORYS

There are stories galore that Harry told, which were probably embellished through time. Harry was a good storyteller; I remember listening to them time and time again. I enjoyed them so much that I couldn't wait for more.

THE SNAKE BITE.

Harry and his mate Timby camped in a shearing shed one cold rainy night. A fire was required to dry their clothes and boil the billy. Wood had to be found and fetched to an area to make a fire that would not destroy the shearing shed. In collecting an arm full of wood and bark a snake was not noticed in the bundle. It poked it's head out and bit Harry on the chest and rib cage area. Naturally Harry had visions of an early departure from this world. Frantically he ordered his mate to get the razor and score the bite area then to suck out the venom. Timby said, "Christ Harry I might kill you". Harry's reply was simple and straight forward. "Timby, if you don't bloody well do it and do it now, I bloody well will die". After the primitive operation was completed, an antiseptic was needed. All that was available was some horse liniment, on went the horse liniment. All hell broke loose with Harry screaming and thrashing about due to the heat the liniment generated. Next morning, they walked with their horse teams in toe to the nearest town in the hope of finding a doctor. The liniment had blistered his chest to the extent that he had to carry the giant blister in his arms. Treatment of some description was carried out on the blister with him surviving the snake bite and horse liniment saga.

EGGIE'S APPLES

One more of Harry's stories which is supposed to be true. It's worth a minute of your time to try and understand the mirth of Harry. One liners were his strength. It's hard to believe but here it is.
Harry was buying 3 pounds of apples from Eggie Smith's milk bar and fruit shop in Rushworth. Eggie couldn't find the right combination of apples to make the 3 pounds exactly. One off, a smaller one on, still not right, do it again. This went on a couple of times, Harry got fed up with Eggie's pondering and said to him.
"For- Christ's sake Eggie take a bite out of one". True story.

STARTING A FAMILY and the MOVE.

Those days must have been very-very hard but Harry and Edna found time to start a family. On 4.9.1931 Doris Eleanor was born followed by Betty Elaine on 8.1.1933. Harry wanted a boy, so Betty was known as Jackie for many years. Another three years passed before Margaret Ethel arrived on 15.2.1936. At this stage and after 8 years of pioneering the property, the government/bank decided that Harry and his uncle were not likely to succeed so they foreclosed the loans. This meant all the sweat and tears, long hours of hardship, little or no money coming in, the venture was a thing of the past.

It was time to pack up and leave Lake Cargelligo and their dream of owning their own farm.

Harry's uncle Ackie had purchased a property at Rushworth in central Victoria. It was now time to move on and set up a new life at Rushworth. Doris was about 5 years old, Betty (Jackie) 3 and Margaret was a baby in arms. The Rushworth property of 362 acres was on the banks of an irrigation channel called the Wyuna. This was ideal to become a dairy farm. An abundance of water with soil being able to be worked to grow pasture, lucerne and crops of wheat, barley, and oats. I believe Harry started share farming with his uncle until he was able to purchase it. Mum and dad called the property Kargell Park. It is assumed after Lake Cargelligo. The name is still used to this day and is displayed on the entrance gate. The farm was situated on Zeglin Road between Middle and McEwan roads approximately five miles plus (9km) north of Rushworth.

From here on is the most interesting part of this story, as on the 13/9/1938 I was born at the Rushworth Bush Nursing Hopspital. I don't remember much about it except that I was right next to mum. Near two years later, the last of Harry's and Edna's children was born. Number five was Graeme John born on 19/7/1940. Now three girls and two boys, just what the doctor ordered. The farm would run like clock work in the coming years.

THE BIRTH OF A BOY (At last someone to help around the farm)

My years 1 to 11.

Ready for work. About 9 y/old

Being born a boy my parents would have been so very happy after the three girls. A boy to grow into a strong youth that could help on the farm. As an infant I spent a lot of time in the dairy as mum milked whilst supervising the kids. As we grew older, naturally, we were introduced to the milking procedures.

By six years old I had moved from the wood heap to milking duties. Wood heap duties was to gather chips, bark and small lumps of wood in preperation for either of the two fires. The open one in the lounge room or the cooking stove in the kitchen . Both fires were important, as mum used the kitchen stove for many things other than just cooking, heating the large kitchen and rear rooms, keeping a supply of boiling water in the kettle, near boiling water in the large fountain on the hob of the stove, heating flat irons for ironing clothes, keeping food warm in the oven and making toast on the wire toasting fork. The lounge room fire was mainly to keep the family warm in the chilly winter months and make toast for supper on the red hot coals, again using the wire toasting fork. This wood heap duty was passed down to Graeme as I became an intricate part of the dairy duties.

Some of my duties were to fetch the cows from the paddocks, helping with the milking of between 30 and 70 depending on the time of the year. At times a percentage of cows would be dried off for a spell prior to them calving. Helping feed the calves and pigs and cleaning up the dairy and milking bails.

The milking was done by a 3 unit Ridd Milking Machine driven by a one cylinder kerosene fuelled engine driving all the milking plant by a series of belts. The "one lung" engine was started with a crank handle hooked on to the fly wheel. When the engine fired you relaxed the grip on the crank handle and it would release. If you got it wrong the crank handle would fly off and belt you in the shins. My late uncle Nobbie could testify to this.

As I grew older, my sisters Doris, Margaret and I could manage the afternoon/after school milking. Betty was "not good" with cows. She would help in the house helping mum. With younger brother Graeme on the wood heap and dad irrigating or the likes, we all had jobs and were gainfully employed.

THE JUNKET for TEA.

This brings to mind a story on Betty's cooking. As we had a plentiful supply of milk it was not uncommon to have milk puddings such as custards, sago, bread and milk and junket. One evening Betty was making a junket, she couldn't get it to taste right. It was discovered that due to poor lighting, a kerosene lamp only, she had laced the junket with sewing machine oil instead of vanilla essence. It's fair to say, the junket was thrown out.

FEEDING THE ANIMALS.

Generally, there would be about 20 calves and 30 pigs to feed. The feeding meant we had to carry numerous five-gallon buckets of whey (separated milk) to either the pigs or the calves. When the calves were young, they were tethered under shade trees called boobiallas. They had to be taught to drink from a bucket, later they were put in the calf paddock. The teaching of young calves to drink was done by putting your fingers in the mouth of the calf which would suck, then push their head into the bucket. Once they got the idea that their feed was in the bucket it was a matter of holding the bucket very firmly as they would push and butt. Pigs were much easier, just pour the whey, skimmed milk, into troughs. The mother sow would teach the piglets to drink from the trough or they would feed from her udder. The reason for separating the milk was to take the cream component out of the milk. The cream was stored in cream cans and picked up two or three times a week by Bill Carmody. Bill would collect from all the farmers and deliver to the Stanhope Butter Factory. It is believed that the cream cheques kept the family for up to three months. At this time all bills would be settled. I have found a diary that states this.

STARTING SCHOOL.

I started school at Stanhope South State School when 6 years and 3 months. It was common to start school after turning 6 if you were born in the last 6 months of the year. If born in the first 6 months, you could start at 5 plus years old. The school was a one teacher school. The teacher was Bob Osborne and generally between 16 and 24 students in grades of one to six attended. At times the grade 5 and 6 kids would help with teaching the grades 1s and 2s. Mrs Osbourne would help at times, particularly with singing and needle work for the girls. The boys did garden work in lieu of needle work.

The trek to and from school was a 3 ½ miles bike ride along a gravel and corrugated road named Middle Rd. At times the cream man, Bill Carmody would give us a lift if he was going straight back to the butter factory. On the way home if we were battling a strong wind, my brother and I would keep our eyes out for Mr Whitaker's gravel truck. If we could see him appearing from behind us, we would pretend we had a chain problem with the bikes. Often, he would throw our bikes on board. With us making room in the cabin, we were soon home.

I distinctly remember my first day at school. My sister Margaret looked after me, getting me to school on time and handing me over to Mr Osborne and school life. Also starting that day was Beth Burnie. She arrived on her little bike with her father Stan on his big black horse Prince. After some small talk it was time to start her school life. There was no way that Beth was going to let her dad ride off and leave her behind. She cried and cried for some time and would not let him go. Finally, Mr Osborne made Beth and me join hands and enter the school leaving her dad behind. We instantly became "a couple".

A lot happened at that little school on the side of an irrigation channel. I learnt to swim in the channel, participated in school sport days, entered in many events even if it was not your thing due to our pupil numbers. In the main it was like all schools of that era, we learnt to read, write, spell, add, subtract, multiply, and divide without calculators, computers or the mobile phone. We also learnt to share things that others didn't have. My footy was shared, a cricket bat or tennis racket was shared and for those where their families could not afford a lunch for them, my mother would make a spare one to share with the less fortunate. To bring such attitude and humanity back into today's teachings would be a blessing.

Looking back to those school days in the little school on the irrigation channel bank were good days. Special days in fact. It's where it all started for me, about eighty long years ago. So much happened going to and from school. If we suffered a puncture or a bike mal function, we would go to Paddy Doyle's farm where his son Hughie would attend to our woes. Doyle's were about ½ mile (700 meters) from the school and very handy for all our problems to be fixed.

If the wind was too strong, Mrs Doyle, a squat white haired real Irish lady would call to her crippled son John, "John take the Fox kids home". The horse and cart would soon be in readiness to throw the bikes in and off we would go.

John was gored by a bull in his teens becoming very crippled. There wasn't much he could do on the farm so driving us home on a few occasions

My headmaster Bob Osborne, wearing glasses.

Some of the many at the back to Stanhope South day.

would have given him some relief from his boredom. He had two older brothers, Pat and Hughie and a younger brother

Jimmy. Unfortunately, their father Paddy was killed on his way home from Hughie's wedding. His truck was housed at our place for quite some time with a fair amount of blood splattered throughout the cabin.

I attended a back to Stanhope South in the late 1970s and soon after, the school was closed, and many stories closed with it. I found two old photos which are shared on the prior page.

THE BIKE TRICK.

On the 700-meter stretch between school and Doyle's corner, some of the kids going south would ride their bikes flat out then jump off to see how far their bike would travel before falling over or crashing into the table drain. My sister Margaret was a solid girl and not too nimble on her feet. One afternoon she tried the "bike trick", stumbling for a meter or so after her jumping off effort. She crash-landed on her knees and slid along the gravel road. What a mess she made of her first jump off trick. Naturally it was into Mrs Doyle for necessary first aid. A good wash out of her nasty gravel rash followed by antiseptic ointment and bandages before John was summoned to yoke up the horse and cart and drive the Fox kids home. No more bike tricks for Margie. Mrs Doyle was a saint.

GRAEME AND HIS HORSE RIDE.

Kerry Forsyth rode a pony to school; he called it Flossy. Again, the kids living south of school would congregate at Doyle's corner prior to Kerry and others dispersing in different directions. Kerry would often offer us a ride on Flossy. One afternoon my young brother Graeme was riding flat out when Flossy shied. Graeme went flying sideways from the saddle landing headfirst into a table drain. Great concern was shown as Graeme lay there motionless. In due course, and to our delight, he opened his eyes, and we were able to continue our trek home. That finished Graeme and his horse riding. Mum and dad would not have been told for fear of repercussions.

Another horse encounter was when Mrs Brown drove a horse and sulky to pick up her young son from school. In the paddock opposite Doyle's were a couple of mares, presumably in season. The horse Mrs Brown was driving could evidently smell the mares and played merry hell. He took off kicking at the sulky, fortunately Mrs Brown and her son either jumped out or was thrown out. The bolting horse galloped between trees and between trees and fence posts smashing the sulky to bits and pieces. If the Browns had not left the sulky when they did the result would have been very different. Maybe a fatality.

THE EVENING MILK

There would be about 10 kids travelling south together, one by one they would peel off to their respective farms. We were the last of the pack and would often have to round up our cows and get them home for their evening milking. If there were none to drive home it was direct home to the kitchen for a piece of bread and jam, change into our farm clothes and down the paddocks to fetch the cows to start milking. By about 7pm the milking, pig and calf feeding, bails washed out and cleaned up. It was now time for tea and homework. On occasions we would catch a bit of Martins Corner or Dad and Dave on the wireless. After tea it was time for homework then into bed for a well-earned sleep, in readiness for it to all start again tomorrow.

PHILLIP GREENAWAY'S SHEEP

One of our neighbours was Phillip Greenaway, he ran a fair few sheep on his property but spent a lot of time away. He lived about 10Kms away in Rushworth. In the lambing season it is essential that ewes are watched and assisted with birthing. I was asked, through my father, to tend his flock. My younger brother helped from time to time. If the ewe was down and couldn't get up, the crows would pick at their eyes and around their back sides. Often it was the case when we had to chase the ewe down and assist in the final part of the birth of a still born lamb. We were primitive Vets at a young age. It was good education for six- and eight-year-olds.

SCHOOL SEX AT 6 YEARS OLD.

Not long after starting school I was assigned to a desk with a young girl of my age. The young girl from a very prominent family (No names, no pack drill) said to me "You show me yours and I'll show you mine". Naturally I was horrified and flatly refused the invitation. My first sexual encounter at the age of six.

Now, it could have resulted in a court case or even a sexual harassment charge.

As mentioned earlier a lot went on in our little school on the banks of the irrigation channel. This same girl was a real tom boy and gave the boys plenty to think about. She was known to visit the boy's toilet or raise the rear trap door, where the pan was removed from for emptying, and thrust a stick or bramble into your bottom. She was a real terror.

MARGARET THE FIGHTER

My sister Margaret was in 5th grade, I was in 3rd grade. Bob Osborne (Mr Osborne in those days) was giving 5th and 6th grades dictation from the school paper. The school paper was sent to all schools in Victoria, I think monthly, and distributed to all students. It was like a learning bible having times tables, spelling lists, arithmetic and reading in it. He said to the students "Read page such and such, the dictation will come from somewhere on those pages. If you have trouble with the spelling of any word, practice it by writing it on your blotter". We used steel- nibbed pens with inkwells situated in the desk centre and the right-hand side, a reason for the compulsory teaching of writing with your right hand. Hence, we used blotting paper known as blotter to dry your writing preventing smudges.

Yes, you have guessed it, Margie wrote a word from the paragraph that old Bob had selected for their dictation. As he was walking around the grades and dictating, he spotted Margie had practiced a word on her blotting paper. He bellowed out, "Margaret Fox you are cheating". Her reply was simple and honest "This is what you told us to do "she said. With a higher, more agitated voice he said, "You're a cheat Margaret Fox". At this stage Margie was getting upset and not taking a backward step retaliated with "I'm not a cheat so shut your bloody trap you". Bob was now furious ordering her out of the school room, which she duly refused. Now the tug of war started, Bob red faced with veins in his neck protruding tried to drag her out of the desk to throw her out. By this time her desk companion had scooted. Ink wells, books, pens and pencils went flying from the desk, but Margie stayed firm in her desk. Bob came to me and asked, "Is she like this at home". I was dumb struck and couldn't find an answer. As this was going on Margie rose from her desk and marched out of the school room and went home leaving Bob in a rage. Naturally she told mum and dad of the fracas. A day or two later there was a School Committee Meeting which dad was a member. Bob was told in no uncertain fashion, "Lay your hands on my daughter again and I'll knock your bloody block off". In today's environment someone might have been jailed.

SCHOOL HOLIDAYS.

For some of the kids, school holidays were holidays. Not so for the Fox kids. Holidays for us were workdays. There were thistles to slash and dig out. There were stones to pick up in the paddocks. There was hay stooking and hay carting. There was lamb marking and de-tailing. I learnt to sow wheat bags, so there was another job in the season. Thistle slashing needs no further explanation except to talk on the method of knowing when it was lunch time or similar and we were in the furthest away paddocks. Mum would hang a white sheet on the clothesline which we could see from any place on the farm. This method of knowing the time was as good as a Rolex watch.

The number of stones was a result of the virginal paddocks being scarified (read ploughed), this stirred the stones to the earth surface where we had to pick them up to form heaps. Dad would follow up with horse and dray and fork the stones into it. Tons of stones were picked up each year.

Stooking hay was the art of drying out the hay sheaves. Sheaves were dropped from the binder/cutter after being bundled and tied then stooked, for drying. Stooking is the standing of 10 or 12 sheaves on their ends to form a Tee Pee for further drying and the ease of loading the wagon. Following the stooking, the sheaves were transported to the stack yard by horse and wagon and built into large stacks.

Lamb marking was the removal of tails from all the lambs and the removal of the male lambs' genitals. This was all done with a very sharp knife, the same knife that Harry cobbled our boots and shoes with. Later, special rubber rings replaced the knife and were placed on the bits to be removed. In time the bits would die and drop off. My job in this exercise was to hold the lamb still on a post for Harry to perform the operation. The dress used to stop the blood from ruining my work cloths was a chaff bag suitably cut with head and arm holes. There was always something to occupy our time, Harry made sure of that. All these chores were done in conjunction with the daily milking and animal feeding. There was no arguing or refusing just get on with it as we knew no other.

My HERCULES AEROPLANE

At about seven I saw my first aeroplane travelling across the sky almost directly above the farmhouse. I can remember that I wanted an aeroplane and

must have pestered mum and dad about it for months. Come Christmas my pestering had paid off. My wish for my own aeroplane was granted. My one and only present was a big red plane resembling a Hercules. It was made of wood and heavy, probably 70 to 90 cms long with a wingspan of similar dimensions. It had only one propeller which would spin if I ran fast enough. I spent hours running around the house yard with the prop spinning.
Not the best Christmas present I ever got but I did ask for it.
Next time I'll ask for a new footy or a motor car but not an aeroplane.

LORD MAYOR'S CAMP

In 1947 I was granted a holiday for disadvantaged children to the Lord Mayor's Holiday Camp at Portsea, south of Melbourne. It was referred to as The Lord Mayor's Prison Farm. Whilst this was a change from farm life it was very regimented with exercise, health checks, organised hikes and swims spread over about 10 days.

On the way home I got quite ill with travel sickness. Bus from Portsea to Spencer St station in Melbourne, train to Murchison and Tiger train to Rushworth. In total we travelled for about 5 ½ hours. My sister Betty met me at the Rushworth station during her lunch break at the high school.

We took my suitcase and belongings to Eggy Smith's café, storing them until my parents came into town. I wandered around waiting for my parents to arrive as they were going to Coyle's auction market. I developed a tummy pain and hot footed to Cootman's hotel toilet situated about 50 meters from the pub. I made about 40 meters down their yard before the accident of all accidents happened.

I locked myself in the cubical and cringed every time I heard footsteps approach. I thought every man visiting the toilet was drunk. Being a farm boy, I was petrified. After about an hour I plucked up the courage to leave the cubical and climb up the wall so I could gain the attention of someone. A gentleman was passing by, so I yelled out to him. "Excuse me do you know my dad". After a bit of toing and froing we established that he knew my father and would try and find him at Coyle's auction and tell him of my problem.

Sometime later my father arrived at the toilet with a wheat bag. He bundled me into it and proceeded to the hotel wash house. Mum was there waiting with a trough full of cold water and in I went. My sister Betty was sent to Eggy Smith's café to find suitable clothing from my suitcase for the final leg

of my Portsea Holiday, home to the farm and my own bed.
Thank goodness that day was over.

COWBOYS No 1

Graeme and I always wanted to be cowboys like the ones at the Kyabram rodeo. It was one of the exciting outings each year. Mum got us each an outfit of leather waist coat, riding chaps, hat, a belt with gun holsters and cap guns. We thought we were big time mixing with the real cowboys, the Le Guard twins, Bluey Potts, Johnny Pearce, Noel Bottoms and many more.

We would often challenge our neighbours, Ross and Alan Murray to calf riding, rodeo style. We got many a cuff from Harry for riding his calves. The Murray boys would run around holding the calf's tails and thought they were rodeo riders. This was not for Graeme and me, we would mount up and hang on for dear life as the calves bolted round and round the calf pen, sometimes through the fence. It was no wonder dad gave us a touch up at times. On one occasion we were double dinking on a fair size bull calf which managed to get up onto sloping roof of their shelter. The calf was frightened to move. We were frightened to get off. Calls for help saw dad arrive giving us both a fair touch up.

COWBOYS No 2.

Sir John McEwan (known as Blackjack) was the Prime Minister of Australia for a short period of about 2 months, after the disappearance of Harold Holt in December 1967 when swimming off Portsea on the Mornington Peninsula, Victoria.

Sir John had numerous properties near us. One was adjacent to us and managed by Eddy Chong, where he ran sheep. The fences between us were not too flash allowing his stud rams to break through to our place. Brother Graeme and I would round them up into the sheep yards and ride them, cowboy style. Sporting a good coat of wool, the rams wouldn't last long before tiring and refusing to move no matter what our persuasion was. Some of our persuasions were a bit cruel as you can imagine. At this point we would endeavour to drive them back to where they had come from. In doing this some would stagger along the fence line and finish in the drainage channel. A few bubbles and never to be seen again as they disappeared to the bottom.

When the water receded in the winter months the carcasses of Blackjack

McEwan's prize rams were quite visible. I can't remember the consequences if any. Yes, we were naughty boys but the chance to have a rodeo, riding these big rams was just too compelling and besides what a story to tell. It was always said "Australians rode on the sheep's back."

MY PET COW TEENA.

Somewhere in my farm life, at about 7 years old, I obtained the most beautiful animal. How she became mine I cannot remembered. We were inseparable as can be seen from my only photo. Teena was a good-sized Jersey. She would find herself at the rear of the herd just so we could walk together on our way to milking or back to the paddocks. She contracted an illness which dad thought was milk fever. I discovered she was down (collapsed) in the shed paddock and could not stand.

Me and Teena

I spent every available free minute with her. We never had a Vet, but dad and I struggled on with her, dad doing what he could to ease her suffering. After a week or so Teena broke my heart, when I went to feed and talk to her, I found her dead. I still get goose bumps when I see the accompanying photo. A sad story but very true, kids on farms attach themselves to anything that gives them joy.

CHURCH

Me, ready for Sunday School and Church

Mum was brought up in the faith of the Methodist Church. As already written earlier, she taught Sunday School, played the organ and was very active in the Corop church where she was married in 1928. On her shifting to Lake Cargelligo the opportunity was not there for her to keep up her faith. With the move to the Rushworth farm, she was able to re-kindle and choose Stanhope Methodists.

Each Sunday we would be dressed up in our best attire and travel the 7 miles. The children would have Sunday

School first, prior to church. At about halfway through the service, the kids were allowed out. We would buy an ice block or ice-cream at the only milk bar in Stanhope before our return home to get ready for the evening milk. An ice block or ice cream doesn't seem much, but to us it was a real treat. It was well worth going to Sunday School and church.

ENTERTAINMENT

As kids we mainly entertained ourselves. We didn't have a lot of spare time, but my brother and I would generally be found together bird nesting, rabbiting, fishing and checking hollow posts for Rosella parrots. If any were found, they would join others in our parrot cage. Other than that, we were like all boys, getting into mischief and trouble, paying the price with getting a wack on the bum. One of these mischievous encounters was trying to catch ducks that visited a dam in the bottom paddock. Graeme and I tied fishhooks onto fishing line baited by big juicy garden worms and tethered it to stakes. We thought this was fool proof and would need to re-bait daily. We had the worms in a paint tin hidden under a fencing stay rail. An inquiring cow put her nose in the paint tin. She must have banged the tin on the ground to free herself but instead imbedded into her flesh. Around and around the paddock she galloped. Dad, Graeme, and I eventually got her into a bail to remove the blessed paint tin. Dad couldn't remove it as it had cut through her flesh and skin into the bone. After much time and swearing he was successful. Much more successful than me and Graeme, we did not catch one duck. Our great intention was a total flop.

Bird nesting was possible cruel as I look at it now. We had a large shed in the corner of the shed paddock. This shed had a very thick hay roof. The hay kept the rain out while making a perfect place for birds to make nests along with possums, mice, and the occasion brown snake. We would rob the nest of eggs depriving the hen of motherhood. The eggs would have a hole put in both ends then by mouth we would blow into the hole forcing the yoke and white out. The shells would be kept for a reason that I can't remember.
Rabbiting was good fun. We had one rabbiting dog, "Bendy", he was called Bendy due to bent legs. He wasn't much good at working stock, so rabbits were his go. We were not allowed to use Rover, dad's dog as that may spoil him for farm work. On occasions we would sneak him out with us. If caught there was the usual punishment. Fishing was generally a Sunday afternoon activity. Good size Red Fin were caught by line in the big hole next to the bridge approximately 60 yards from our back door.

We were always kicking a footy or playing a match against the Murray boys. A rub down was necessary after an hour or so. Dad would generally do it, but his hands were just too rough and could remove skin within minutes. Our outings were simple. Dances and euchre parties with our parents at the school, Sunday School, and church at Stanhope Methodist church. Of course, there was always Aussie Rules footy on Saturdays in the winter months. We followed Stanhope in the Goulburn Valley League and loved our day out.
 I have been told and can vaguely remember that I would play the opposition by myself from the boundary line taking marks, kicking goals, running, and tackling as well as barracking. By the time we returned home I had done a day`s work and was exhausted. I was generally excused from milking duties and put to bed. On the Saturdays when we went to footy, the milking would start about 2 hours late and finish well into the dark. Somehow, we managed under lanterns as electricity was never connected to the property during our ownership. It came much later.

HARRY and Mrs PERRY
One Saturday when entering the Stanhope ground in the 1936 Pontiac that Harry had recently purchased, Mrs Perry was walking in front of us dodging potholes and puddles. In her possession was a lovely cream sponge for the canteen. As Harry was passing her, she side stepped a puddle and was hit in the bum with the right-hand head light. She jumped up in the air in fright before landing on the mudguard and sliding to the ground into a muddy pothole. The sponge went flying and a hungry dog took the opportunity to grab the sponge and flee. Unfortunately, Mrs Perry must have fallen the wrong way and broke her wrist. There was hell to play over it for the rest of the day which carried on for weeks if not months. I'm not sure of the outcome but I do know that the dog ran away with the cake.

MUM AND THE KETTLE FAMILY
It was a wet and muddy day, we went to the football at Stanhope in the "T" Model Ford small truck, our only means of transport. Kids in the back under a cover of wheat bags, mum, and dad in the front. During the match sister Margaret felt ill with a cold/flu, she retreated to the back of the "T" Model snuggling down under the bag cover. Soon after she was teased by the Kettle girls. Margie couldn't put up with it so climbed out to tell mum of her problem. Mum had to protect her daughter by chastising the Kettle girl, this

didn't go down too well with Mrs Kettle so she tackled mum with a push and a shove. Mum arked up with her own push, shove, and a few words. Next thing it was on. Two women in full combat with each other.

As for who won the contest, that didn't really matter as Margie was left alone to suffer in silence. The two women returned to the footy match with their pride somewhat in tatters.

ENTERTAINMENT AT THE SCHOOL

The dances and euchre at the school allowed the kids of the time to play ghost games in the dark or postman's knock in the shelter shed. I can't remember the rules to postman's knock except at some stage you were paired with the opposite sex and sent out into the dark. You were supposed to have a kiss or two, I never got to kissing, possibly I didn't know how or was too embarrassed, we would just hold hands. Things change as you get older. Thank goodness!

Catching frogs and frightening the hell out of the Hudson girls was another game we played. One night the bigger boys in grades 5 and 6 and I caught a very big ugly frog and sneaked it into the school hall. At the right time they placed it in front of Jeanie (Crackers) Hudson. A hop and a squark from the frog and Crackers went berserk. Tables and people were knocked everywhere. A real fracas. We thought that this was great entertainment, something you would pay big money to witness. A great bit of fun until Monday morning when the guilty ones were called to account. A lecture on how, why, when and who, with behaviour standards and punishment was thrown in. It resulted in the big kids getting the cane and I along with other deemed little kids escaped punishment except for the lecture.

HAY CARTING TIME. (Sheaved hay

A Binder

By the time I was 7 or 8, dad thought I was big and strong enough to help with the hay carting. Firstly, dad would reap the oats with a binder. This was a machine drawn by horses that would cut the oats with a 4-to-5-foot blade. As the hay was cut it would fall onto a tray and be propelled through canvas sheets and rollers. The oaten hay would all lay in the same direction heads together and butts together. When sufficient hay to make a sheaf was rolled through the rollers it would be automatically tied with hay-band (twine) and dropped to the ground.

After allowing time for the hay to dry out, stooking was the next phase.

After stooking (standing the sheaves up like a tee pee) the oaten sheafed hay would be left to further dry. When right to stack I would work the wagon building the load, dad would pitch the sheaves to me until the wagon was full. There was a special way to load the wagon. Each row of sheaves had to bind the previous row in. By doing this the load could be extended. More sheaves on meant less trips therefore less time. If there was poor binding and part of the load fell off, I would cop some type of punishment. You only made the mistake once.

Often after the last couple of sheaves were to be loaded a big brown snake would emerge from beneath, sporting a belly full of mice, quite fierce and very deadly if bitten. You could see the formation of the mice in its belly. Many a pitchfork handle was broken in the demise of brown snakes. After the wagon was full it was off to the stack yard. The wagon was drawn by 2 or 3 Clydesdale horses. Harry didn't believe in tractors, too much to go wrong. It was easier to throw some hay and chaff to the horses. They never break down was his theory.

He would set the corners for a sheaf haystack, and I would build it as he tossed sheaf after sheaf to me. To prevent water from entering the sides and roof of the stack, the stack is sloped out from bottom to top before it changes direction to form the sloped roof. This would continue until all the hay was in. It would take days and weeks to get it all done. A stack could be any size, we would let the yield dictate the size. Some years there would be two stacks. A stack would measure around 30 feet by 12 feet and 12 feet high. (10m x 4m x 4m high)

HAY CARTING. (Baled hay)

Baled hay was a lot different. We would get contractors in to do the baling after Harry had cut the lucerne with a 4 feet wide horse drawn mower, raked it into wind rows and then the wind rows into cocks. This was done with a hay rake pulled by a horse. The hay rake had half rounded tines. When the rake was full a hand leaver was pulled to release the roll of hay. This would make the wind rows. By raking along the wind row, this would form the cocks. After drying for a few days, the contractors would arrive with the baler and sweep.

The sweep was attached to the front of a truck. It was a series of long wooden or metal fingers pushed by the truck along the ground pushing the cocks to a central point where the baler was situated. The baler was driven by a stationary tractor drive pulley and belts. The lucerne would be pitch forked into the baler and compressed into bales of about 3 feet long by 15 x 15 inches. The bales were automatically tied with special wire or twine. Bales would weigh 50 to 70 lbs (30 to 50 Kgs) depending on the type of grass being baled.

As the bales were spat out the rear of the baler, they would be stacked in preparation for carting in.

Now days with modern equipment, the cutting and compressing into bales is done in the one motion. The cut is much wider, up to 10 meters being done by electronics using the principles of the GPS. With equipment like this much bigger paddocks of hundreds of acres can be harvested in record times.

I was about 10 years old and can distinctly remember the day I was up about 10 feet on top of the load, Harry threw me a real green bale, I threw my hook out to pull it onto the load. Being a green bale, it was much heavier, too heavy for me. Me and the bale landed at Harry's feet. He grumped at me "Nevie, stop buggerizing and get back up". I copped a kick up the bum to keep my mind on the job. He was a hard man.

All work on the farm was done with horses being the main means of muscle. Tractors were not considered. We had three strong Clydesdales, Lofty, Noble and Dick with Kate making up the main team. We also had Bess when required but she was mainly used in the spring cart and dray cartage. Years earlier there was Jerry, he was used in the sulky and gig. Mum used Jerry to do the shopping in Rushworth prior to the T model Ford light truck.

Whilst dad was tough, strong, and hard on us kids he liked telling stories and taking the pee out of others. The following very true story might emphasise this.

PANSIE.

One Monday morning I had to go back to the milking shed and help prior to my 3 ½ mile bike ride to school. Mum was suffering a migraine, being looked after by Betty. She was house duties as she seldom helped in the dairy. I was all dressed up for school in clean overalls and shirt. We only had two good pair of overalls, one on and one in the wash.

There were only a few cows to be put through the milking process. The cows had been on fresh clover during the night, to say the least, they were a bit loose. A yellow jersey named Pansie strolled into her bail and started munching on chaff in the feed box. She lifted her tail to indicate a bowel rumbling, I grabbed the square mouth shovel to catch the spill, when because of chaff going down the wrong way, she coughed and a stream from Pansie's bowel hit me square in the face. My mouth, nose, eyes and ears were full of Pansie's movement, my clean overalls and shirt were drenched.

Harry saw this as hilarious and was laughing his head off while he flushed me with a 5-gallon pale of water. This made the green matter spread further down to my boots. He sent me home to get cleaned up. Mum had one look at me and was violently ill leaving Betty to try and clean me up.

After a lot of scrubbing, digging and gouging, she gathered last weeks' dirty school clothes as there were no others. I was now ready to ride the 3 ½ miles to school except I needed a note for being late. Harry scribbled one and off I pedalled. I presented myself and note to old Bob, a grin then a big laugh come from Bob after reading Harry's note. I reckon he would have written something like "Please excuse Nevie for being late as Pansie sh** on him". I smelt like a farm dairy, consequently I sat by myself and played by myself as the other kids couldn't stand the stench of me or the colour of my skin, pink with a tinge of green.

YOU CAN RUN BUT YOU CAN'T HIDE.

Mum took some pride in her garden of vegetables and flowers. Dad had connected some one- inch pipes to run water from the tank on one side of the house to her gardens on the opposite side. The pipes were temporarily laid across wooden boxes and kerosene drums to get the right fall for the water. This day dad was talking to the baker who delivered once a week. I was bouncing up and down on the strategically placed water pipes. Not wanting to show his anger toward me, he called out "Nevie get off those bloody pipes". I kept bouncing, more orders to get off were uttered but I kept bouncing, as I was safe as long as the baker was present. Finally, the baker left, I knew I was to get corporal punishment for the bouncing and for disobeying, I took off with dad in pursuit. Through mum's garden trampling down my pumpkin patch and out the front gate. I could outrun dad and had a comfortable advantage of about 20 metres. Mum saw and heard the goings on and shouted, "Harry let him go, he'll have to come home to eat".

I stayed out of site for hours missing the milking and animal feeding. It became very dark, and the night sounds started, horses rolling, cows bellowing, owls hooting, curlews calling to name a few. I wasn't too frightened as I was fairly used to the dark and night noise, but I was hungry. It dawned on me that mum was right, I had to go home to eat and face the music. I crept in through the back door and sat on my chair. Harry flew out of his chair and gave me the belting of all beltings for disobeying, not helping with the milking and anything else he could think of. I can still hear him saying "You'll eat off the bloody mantel piece for a month by the time I finish with you". My bum was so sore, the mantel piece seemed a good idea. Mum ordered me to bed without tea. Life was tough but survive we did.

GRAEME'S FLIRT WITH DEATH.

Another story that is worth a mention. My little brother Graeme and I were playing on the veranda, he was about 3 and me about 5. I would put him in the old pram and push him down the veranda which was about 30 feet long. After the push I would run after it and catch it before it hit the bathroom wall. We had done this many times but this time I left my sprint to stop it a little late. Crash, bang the pram handle went straight through the weatherboard wall. Graeme hit his head front and back. My sister Margaret seeing Graeme vomiting etc was off to get mum from the cow shed. Before she left, I said to her, "Don't tell mum I'm hiding behind the kitchen door". Mum raced in with a stick, ripped the kitchen door back to find me crouched and scared. Whack, whack, whack until the stick broke. Thanks, Margie for keeping a secret.

It was thought that Graeme was in a bad way, so mum and dad bundled him into the T model Ford and rushed him to a Rushworth doctor. The doctor said that Graeme was in convulsions and to take him to Mooroopna as he was retiring for the night. Harry evidently went ballistic at this nonsense, for two reasons. Firstly, the doctor had put a dressing gown over his suit, which could be easily seen, he was entertaining guests. Secondly, if Graeme was that sick the 55-mile drive taking near to 90 minutes may have ended Graeme's short life. Harry grabbed the doctor, probably by the throat, and said "If the young fella dies, I'll bloody well come after you and Christ help you". The doctor quickly changed his stand and Graeme was attended to. He survived the ordeal thank goodness or I might have been on a charge of murder at the age of 5 and Harry cracking rocks in the prison for verbal abuse, malicious injury and maybe manslaughter.

LITTLE WHITE LIES.

It doesn't pay for parents to tell little lies to their children even if it is in their best interests.

Our house on the farm at Rushworth was on the bank of a swift flowing irrigation channel. As kids, we were told not to go near it unless we were fishing with an adult. To hammer the point home, mum told us that alligators lived in the channel. Dad told us there were bunyips living under the bridge. On evenings when the horses were rolling in the dirt making a noise, he would say "Listen, can you hear the bunyips in the channel". We were frightened of these monsters particularly with them living on our doorstep. The stories kept us well away from the hazard that both mum and dad may have thought would take our lives.

My brother Graeme and I thought of a way to get friendly with the "monsters". As one of our chores was to feed the chooks and gather the eggs, we decided that we could feed the monsters on eggs and the occasional chook. When collecting the eggs, we would give mum 4 or 5 telling her that the chooks weren't laying. We kept the remaining 14 or 15 and threw them over the fence into the channel for the alligators to eat and hopefully spare us. Clucky chooks were put in a bag for a few days, this was thought it would cure them being clucky. We would throw the bag and clucky chook into the channel from the bridge for the bunyip. This kept going for some time until an accident with the barb wire fence dramatically changed things.

Whilst hurling the eggs into the channel I hooked the back of my right hand on the barb wire. I sliced a deep cut, blood was everywhere. Naturally I went to mum with my problem and of course she wanted to know what caused my injury. I had to confess to the feeding of Bunyips and Alligators. Mum probably felt bad for telling us that little white lie that possibly caused my injury. Mum called Dr Whittaker on our phone that a Mr Kinsman had recently installed. Our number was Rushworth 131. The line wasn't too clear when she told him of my injury. He told her that it would be fine in a day or two but if she was at all concerned to bring me in at the end of the week. By Saturday it was a real mess, festered and full of puss. When Dr Whittaker saw my predicament, he said to mum. "I thought you said he had cut the back of his head. There is only skin there and it would heal quickly". The injury to my hand required the pruning of dead flesh and stiches.

If my memory is correct, there was no chastising for throwing the eggs and cluckey chooks into the channel as my parents had told the fib that caused the lack of eggs and my injury.

DAD'S FLANNELS AND MUM'S FORGIVENESS.

In the areas of Rushworth, Murchison, and Tatura there were several internee camps where the government imprisoned migrants from countries in war with Australia during WW2. Camps 3 and 4 were about 2 miles from our farm, housing mainly people from the Baltic countries that were involved in the war. On occasions these prisoners would be marched to the channel near our place for a swim. There would be 100 or more in each group and guarded by 5 or 6 guards. Somehow some of the guards got to know us and would visit us on Sunday afternoons. They would bring us stuffed toys and lollies for the kids and clothing for dad. On one visit they brought him some flannel shirts. Dad wasn't too happy with them as they were second hand, not washed and displayed soiling and stains on the tails. Once mum washed them, he wore them for years in both summer and winter. Their visits on Sundays didn't do much for mum. They were useless, couldn't or wouldn't help with the milking, animal feeding or cut some wood. Feeding 3 or 4 soldiers as well as a family of 7 took some doing. Mum never refused them a free meal as I suppose she thought they needed company just like we needed.

THE WATER BAILIFF

Mr Armstrong was our water bailiff. He would ride his bike along the channel banks looking for illegal use of the water system whilst checking the water meter on water wheels. He would always get morning tea at our place, if late, he would get lunch. On one occasion he pulled our illegal drum net out and checked it for any fish. He reported "No Fish Harry". Drum nets were illegal. They were made of wire netting with a funnel allowing fish to swim in but prevented them escaping. There was a hefty fine for illegal netting and for chocking the water wheel so free water would be received for irrigation purposes.

Harry along with all other farmers were up to all the tricks under the sun to obtain free water. I often wondered if the morning teas and lunches were a trade-off by dad for his constant use of free water through the chocked water wheel.

OBTAINING IRON BARK

Once a year dad would yoke up two horses in the wagon and travel to the Rushworth Forest to get a supply of Iron Bark, a great substitute for wood. We would use it in the open fire to quell the freezing winter temperatures. Central Victoria gets scorching hot in summer, but winter is the opposite. You could have temperatures below freezing to 14 or 15 degrees above. I would go with him leaving very early to travel about 12 Kms to and 12 Kms home arriving much after dark. It was a long day. Mum would pack us a hearty lunch with a few bottles of cold tea. A water bag was also a must. The Iron Bark is a very thick bark obtained from the trunks of Iron Bark trees which the Rushworth Forest was famous for. The trees were felled and cut into fence posts or for anywhere a hard, lasting timber was required. On the trip home we would ride on the wagon shafts or walk as the load was quite high. Fortunately, that was one day of the year when we weren't wanted in the dairy. Mum and the other kids took control of the milking.

SELLING THE RUSHWORTH FARM,

The Rushworth farm was sold in either 1949 or 1950. I believe it was sold for two reasons. Firstly, Dad had bought a new pedigreed bull, a jersey named Oakington Golden Reflection. It was thought this bull brought a disease with him which caused cows to abort their calves thus destroying the herd. Secondly, the 3 girls needed employment. Doris had already left to become the head cook in the Kyabram hospital at age 16 after a short stint at Cottrell's butcher shop in Rushworth. Betty found a job at Emmett's Store in Stanhope. Doris rode 5 miles south to Cottrell's and Betty 7 miles north to Emmett's along Middle Road, an unmade and corrugated road.

Whatever the reason was, we shifted to Elmore after selling the farm, where we stayed with my uncle Howard Hicks. Howard was mum's brother. I and my brother Graeme attended Elmore primary school for a few months before shifting on to Castlemaine. My teacher was Mr Pointer. This was vastly different to what I was used to. Grades were bigger with a teacher for every grade. We played inter school sports with Goornong. I excelled in football and joined Elmore's 2nds. Elmore players were between 10 and 18 years of age and received a hammering each game. This didn't dampen our enthusiasm as we trained each week in readiness for the next encounter which was generally against grown men.

I had my 12th birthday at Elmore before moving on to Castlemaine where mum and dad had purchased the Tarax Bar and milk bar/café. I think this was mum's idea to go into business, a profession she had missed since her Corop days many years ago. It was also to give a job and training for Betty and Margaret. Doris had already left home continuing at the Kyabram hospital.

The shop was long hours with all of us having to chip in. Dad wasn't too keen on shop life and spent a lot of his time at his parent's farm at Guildford which is about 10 miles from Castlemaine. Later he purchased the farm from his family.

You can take the man out of the farm, but you can't take the farm out of the man.

The Rushworth property was sold to a chap from Murchison that new little about farming. He on sold to the Zeglins then on to the Thorley family. On visiting the farm prior and on the day of the family reunion at Rushworth, I was appalled at the state of the place. Junk and mess everywhere. Admittedly he milks about 700 cows twice a day. You would think he would take pride in his business. Very disappointed, Harry and Edna would turn in their graves to see such a mess.

WILLIAMSTOWN HOLIDAY

My two aunties, Ruby, and Mabel along with my father Harry took four of us to Williamstown in Melbourne for our first holiday other than a weekend at Grandma's, or Lucas's at Corop. We had a house in Ferguson St Williamstown, close to a station, North Willy I think, and near the town hall and picture theatre. The beach wasn't too far away via a viaduct. We had quite a few outings. A trip into Melbourne on a train, my first train ride, a Pantomime where we sat in a VIP box high up next to the stage. I think we saw Robin Hood. George Formby at the Exhibition Buildings rings a bell. Harry took me to the Newport Glass Factory where he spent some time blowing bottles by mouth. Visiting piers was a nightmare with our aunties making sure we walked down the very middle. They thought we would fall into the ocean. That still is vivid in my memory. We were allowed to visit the beach by ourselves after a couple of accompanied visits. On one occasion I lay in the sun for too long and got very sunburnt. I developed blisters and during the night they burst. I was sharing a bed with my sister Betty. I was woken during the night being accused of wetting the bed.

Years 12 to 15.

After arriving at Castlemaine, I spent 3 months at Castlemaine South Primary school completing grade 6 under Mr Williams, a real mean man that didn't mind roughing up his pupils. The following year,1951, I moved on to secondary school at the Castlemaine Technical school. I was never a class A student, spending my time in either the lower A or B section of the forms. I didn't have too much trouble with schoolwork but was forced to leave after form 3, Junior Tech Certificate level. More of that story later.

I played football with the school team, Castlemaine 3rds and Chewton 2nds as well as tennis and school athletics. The fascinating activities in that part of my life was learning to dance at the Campbells Creek fire station, Tom Ottery's Barn and the small schools spread throughout the district. It was at these dances that I found out about the opposite sex. **GIRLS.** The "Creek" fire station dance was a one man show. Laurie McClauson would play the piano from 8pm to midnight, he barely looked at the keyboard and had a continuous smile, great musician, great memories.

Tennis at 11 or 12

Tom Ottery's Barn was an actual shearing shed, taken over by the Castlemaine Pipe Band for the night. When required, it was cleaned out for their use. The Pipers and Drummers would stand in the holding pens and played a series of Scottish dances such as The Gay Gordons, Strip the Willow and The Dashing White Sargent, a few others that escape my memory. The traditional dances were played by Bill and Les Davies, neither of them could read music but with Les on the squeeze box and Bill on guitar each night was a packed shearing shed. Bill and Les played at all the small country schools and small halls.

Les and I were best mates and got up to plenty of mischief over the years. I'm not telling any of those stories. Les passed away a year or so ago at 82. A great mate. Our mischief will be my secret forever. Rest easy buddy.

Chapter 3

FAMILY BREAKDOWN.

In about 1953 my parents parted. The shop was sold, and mum went to work in hotels as a maid. She hated that job, but money was money. She later got a job at the Castlemaine Woollen Mill as a cloak room attendant. The children stayed with mum in the family home at 6 Forest St Castlemaine. Dad spent most of his time at the Guildford farm and in Bendigo with his sisters.

He became a fruit hawker travelling the Victorian roads in his truck accompanied by his dog. He sold apples and pears to the north and oranges and soft fruit to the south of Victoria. It is understood that he made a good living and made strong friends in this venture.

As time passed so did the stance to distance myself from my father. Things happen between couples; my mother and father were no different. Who was right and who was wrong became a "no" subject with me?

I have a saying which accepts the fact that **"every family has one", meaning, a problem within the family.**

I spent time with both, although limited. Nevertheless, my children found they had both a grandmother and a grandfather. Right up to his death in 1985, three years after mum, I would visit him in the aged home in Castlemaine. He was a hard old bugger, bringing us up like his childhood where hard work was a natural. I copped plenty and was taught some values, a lot different to today's youngsters.

MY FIRST DAYS OF WORK,

In 1953 Mum told me that I had to find a job as there was insufficient money coming in to keep the three that were still living at home. There went my school days regardless of my ambitions. She insisted I find a job in a government organisation where you had security, something she never had, and paydays were every fortnight regardless. I sat for entrance exams with all government services. The armed forces, railways, electricity commission and PMG. With no results I started at the Post office as a JPO delivering telegrams just prior to Xmas of 1953. Telegrams were the in thing in that era, especially Xmas wishes. I would ride many miles each day on the traditional heavy postal bikes. One evening at about 6pm a telegram came through for me, it was from the PMG. (Post Master General. Now read Telstra). I had passed the entrance exam to become a Technician in Training, later to be known as a TIT.

Mum and I had one trip to Melbourne to find out where I was to start trainingls. It was the Batman Street Training School in West Melbourne. We had an interview with George Pile, the Welfare Officer, he was able to give us a couple of addresses where I could get lodgings.

We chose 35 Royal Parade Parkville as it was the easiest for me to find my way in a big city. I could walk to the training school via Peel St and the Victoria Markets, across the Flagstaff Gardens to Batman St and the training school. There was an annex to the Batman school in Dudley St, one street away. It was here where we did most of our trade work training.

Mrs Borne was the owner of the boarding house which housed about 50 boarders. She promised us the world but, in the end delivered basic board and measured food for a cost of four pounds a week.

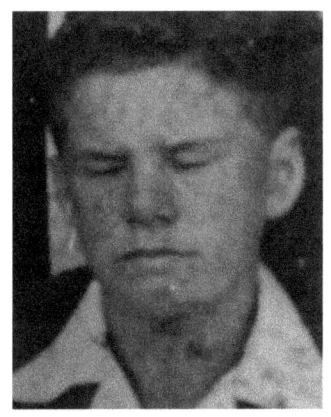
My PMG file photo 1954

After securing my digs it was into the city to buy some clothes. We went to London Stores on the corner of Bourke and Elizabeth streets. It was the only store that mum had heard of, and we purchased my first set of decent clothes including jacket, trousers, shirt and tie. Something that I had never owned. Then back to Castlemaine to wait for 25/1/1954, my start day in the work force **with pay.**

A SCARED KID.

On Sunday the 24/1/1954 mum dropped me at Brown's Hotel, on the corner of Bell Street and Sydney Road Coburg. It was about 6pm when she put me on a tram heading to the city to my boarding house at 35 Royal Parade. I was a petrified 15years and 3 months old boy from the bush on my first tram ride alone. I was pitched into the unknown, I had no idea where to get off. All I knew that the Royal Melbourne Hospital was my landmark. If I reached that I had gone too far. I sat and watched for this tall building. Finally, after about 20 minutes it was there in front of me. I scrambled from the tram with my suitcase and walked back along Royal Parade looking for number 35.

I walked for two blocks to number 35. A sheepish, timid knock on the door, Mrs Borne answered and ushered me to an upstairs room to share with Graeme Scarborough. Graeme was from Bendigo, and we got on very well. I don't think I slept a wink that night as I had to have my first boarding house breakfast of measured quantities, something I was not used to, then find my way to the training school which was about a three-kilometre walk past the Victoria Market and through the Flagstaff gardens.

BOARDING HOUSE LIVING

Numerous stories can be told when living with fifty co-boarders with 50% of them being PMG (Telstra) trainees. I can share a few with you but not all of them as some are best left in the closet.

Number 1 story.

I was ill with a fever; my room- mate called a doctor for a house call. The doc prescribed medication to be taken every 2 hours. My roommate, a university student and sitting exams at that time, sat up all night bathing my forehead and administering the medication. He duly sat and passed his exams.

Neither the landlady nor her staff bothered to check in on me during the days I was ill. No cup of tea etc. Two older ladies made sweets for me at their work. The boys brought me breakfast and evening meals. Fortunately, I was up and about after about a week. Without the comradery I would have been in trouble as the landlady was only after the dollars.

Number 2 story.

There were Chinese uni students occupying 4 or 5 rooms in the boarding house. One evening they had a meeting with other students in one of their rooms. There was a swastika flag on the wall and some anti Australian talk going on. This riled some of the boys and all hell broke out.

After the ruckus ceased, Noel Reynolds put a notice in the toilet with derogative remarks referring to the practice of the male Chinese students standing on the toilet seat when doing their No 2. He signed the notice, Mrs Borne land lady. This caused a hell of a stink resulting for Noel to be evicted on the spot. He knew people a few doors down the street who bunked him for a night or two.

Number 3 story.

Ross Turner loved telling stories which he made up as he told them. One night he was running a bath while telling one of his fib stories and forgot about his bath. When someone left his room for a toilet break, water was found to be running down the carpeted hallway. The fib story was cut short, and we all shot off to bed as the land lady was on the war path after being alerted to water running down the walls below. Again, all hell broke loose as Mrs Borne was after the culprit, checking all rooms and discovering us innocently in bed. Finally, Ross owned up and explained that he ran the bath but fell asleep forgetting all about his bath. Another fib. The story must have been believed as Ross was not thrown out, but his fib stories stopped.

Yes, boarding house life was hard but a lot of fun was had. Some activities can be told, others can't.

Number 4 story.

The boarding house did not have a lounge per-se for the "inmates", we were allowed access to the landladies with certain conditions. The lounge was situated in the front of the building very adjacent to the footpath. People walking past could see in and hear, if the windows were open

There was a pianola complete with rolls. Rolls are special paper on a spindle with a series of holes in the paper. Under the pianola are peddles, when the peddles are pumped air is passed through the holes which provides the piano notes of the tune. Down the side of the roll the words of the song are written. On some Sundays we would have an audience watching from the street as we pumped and sang our lungs out. Whether or not we were thought as musicians, we enjoyed ourselves. My favourite song was "Blue Moon", that received applause on many occasions from the footpath audience.

THE START OF AN ERA.

My introduction to the training school on my first day was with over 200 lads like me. We were lectured on many things, signed lots of forms, pushed into groups, meeting instructors and more. It was a very harrowing day for a 15-year-old bush kid.

The reason for the high intake of trainees in 1954 (500 in total) was to be ready for the next generation of technology. The introduction of automatic switching in every exchange in Australia and the rotary dial, thus doing away with magneto and common battery technology. "Number please, 3 minutes are you extending" uttered by telephonists was to be phased out.

Following my first day of paid schoolwork, it was, find your way home and wait for tea. Measured out helpings of very ordinary food, no seconds like there was at home. We got a sweet, at least that helped fill the gap. Naturally you would expect supper. The answer was **NO** unless you had a cake cooked by your mum when last you were home. This happened to me after telling mum that we were only half fed. I soon had many friends at the boarding house wanting for a slice of mum's lovely fruit cake. If you had unlimited money, you could go next door to The Royal 33 cafe for toasted raisin bread and coffee. About 2 shillings (20cents). Incidentally we had to do our own washing, supply our lunch and one meal each day at weekends. I grew up fast, learning to wash, iron and mend. Ron Stephenson learnt the hard way. He put all his washing in the copper together. The result was multi coloured clothes and very small jumpers.

My Monday to Friday lunches consisted of a bottle of milk which I bought from the canteen at morning teatime and would have a small sip. Lunch time was most of the bottle as saving it for afternoon tea was not always a good idea as I had to store it in my metal locker. In the hot months the locker was like an oven. Often by 3pm I would have a substance like blancmange. No afternoon tea that day.

The question may be asked, "Why not buy a meat pie or bread roll". The answer to that is easy, I could not afford it. My salary was 13 pounds 10 shillings and one penny per fortnight gross. ($27.01) It may sound OK for that era but for the board, tax and superannuation which had to be deducted. Board was eight pounds ($16.00), tax and super about 4 pounds. ($8.00) I was left with three pounds ($6.00) to pay for lunches, fares, entertainment, and the train home to Castlemaine every 2 to 4 weeks. A return train fare to Castlemaine was seventeen shillings and six pence. ($1.75). A Living Away from Home Allowance was paid to country trainees after they were made permanent. I required dental work which prevented the Living Away Allowance being paid for nine months. Eventually I was paid the extra few dollars which helped to a point. There were no pay rises until such time you had eaten up the allowance. This generally occurred during 3rd year.

HITCH HIKING AND THE CHRISTIES.

My main way of travel to and from Melbourne was via the thumb, hitch hiking. I did many miles this way. One driver let me drive his Vanguard while he had a sleep. I had just met him roadside at Essendon where all hitch hiking commenced travelling north on the Calder Highway toward Castlemaine and Bendigo. This wouldn't happen today for obvious reasons.

Mum helped as much as she could, particularly with the lovely fruit cake each time I went home. The first 9 plus months of my working life was pretty tight. I continued at the boarding house for about 2 years until I found private board with Don Christie's family in Mountfield St Brunswick. Whilst Mrs

Christie (Glad) was a nice soul, she loved a punt on Saturdays with the SP bookie. This was illegal but everyone bet with them. I was charged 3 pounds ($6.00) a week. This included seconds, supper if required, all meals, washing and ironing. Much better than the boarding house.

The trouble was with Mr Christie (Dave). He was a big drinker hence there were numerous fights and arguments within the family. Not a good way to live but I was grateful for being taken in by Glad. Don and I played football together, went to dances, picked up the girls. We were good mates doing everything good mates do. It's a shame that time has passed, and Don and I have lost contact. I will put finding him on my bucket list.

Chapter 4

TRAINING. 15 TO 18 YEARS OLD

Me at about 17

Training was over 5 years like the majority of apprenticeships. Our first year was all training schoolwork with a lot of theory, Electricity AC/DC, Magnetism, Mathematics (various), Communications local and long distance, combined with practical subjects. We had 3 or 4 small stints in an exchange during our first year. Second year was slightly different; we spent a month in "class" and a month in the field. At last, we seemed to be getting somewhere.

Third and fourth years were more time in the field. During the 1956 Olympics I was sent to the North Melbourne Subs Installation depot to replace their technicians who were working on communications at various Olympic venues. As I was in 3rd year, I was a boss, not knowing this was to happen to me big time in years to come.

For our field training we would be sent to cover various disciplines in the suburbs and throughout the state. I spent time at Geelong, Daylesford, Seymour, and Bendigo as well as metropolitan areas. During these years we would make our choice to what discipline we would like. Some were lucky and got their choice. I chose Exchange Installation and got it. I stayed in this discipline for 34 years advancing through the ranks from technician to acting branch manager. More of this later.

The fifth year we were assigned to our chosen or given discipline.

Each year of training there were exams to be passed with a pass mark of 60%. Terms were of 4 months with an exam. Just like school.

A failure could be rectified with further tuition and a further exam. Too many failures would mean termination of employment or an assistant technician position. Fortunately, I managed to get a pass each year although some exam results were close to the wind. I was not the brightest trainee but kept at it to forge an interesting and worthwhile career.

FOOTBALL.

The country trainees wanted a football side to play in. Through the welfare officer, a Mr George Pile, a side was formed to play in the Melbourne Boys League. Our colours were blue with white cuffs and collar. I had the honour of being appointed the captain. Later, I became the unofficial coach as no one was appointed in that roll. It was given to any adult that turned up on the day.

The school principal, Mr Bill Chapman, was often used in any capacity including coach, goal umpire or trainer. Bill and I picked the team every Friday. We got on really well, at times I think he may have helped me over the line in a couple of exams. Not many games were won but it didn't seem to bother us. We played matches all over Melbourne on Saturday mornings. We would travel to Burnley, Brighton, Port Melbourne, Carlton, Brunswick, and Hawthorn, to name a few.

I took my brother Graeme to a game at Hawthorn's Glenferrie oval. We were short of players so Graeme was rung in, playing under a dodgy name. Unfortunately, he broke his arm which caused an amount of worry and concern. It was found out later that he could have turned in bed doing the same damage. He was diagnosed with a type of bone cancer that affected him for years. It's still a problem at times even now at 80 years plus. There was no trouble from the football league over the dodgy name/player. Probably thought enough damage had already been done.

I was selected in the combined Melbourne Boys team to play Geelong Boys at Geelong. On the bus I sat with a little bloke called Bobby Skilton. Bobby was representing South Melbourne fourths. He went on to great heights winning 3 Brownlow medals and coaching Melbourne in the VFL/AFL. My success was nowhere near that of Bobby Skilton. I went to Carlton in 1956 and 1957 playing in the 3rds. I trained with the 1st and 2nd sides with Ken Hands, George Ferry, Johnny James, and Peter Webster to name a few. Sergio Silvagni was my captain in 1957. He went on to play 239 games for Carlton. To be brutally honest, I was not good enough but had a red-hot go.

TO DROP A NAME

I must drop the name of Ronald Dale Barassi. The legend of AFL as a player and coach. He was born on the property next door to mine in Guildford Vic.

When he coached Carlton, I was selected by Keith Mills assistant secretary at Carlton to coach a feeder side and would become the 4th coach at Carlton. This did not eventuate for "political reasons." Where might I have ended up? Not bad for not playing 1st grade AFL. A bit more on football later.

The political reasons were twofold.

Firstly, the Northern District League chiefs decided after receiving complaints from possible opponents that we would have had too great a start with success being continuous. The players would have been recruited from all over Victoria and possible Nationally. There would have been adequate funds from Carlton, medical personnel, equipment, the works.

Secondly, the Carlton 3rds coach was on shaky ground and did not want me having input to both 3rds and 4ths as it was ideal for both groups to train together. The 3rds were under nineteen and the 4ths were under seventeen. As stated earlier, where might I have ended up. ??

Chapter 5

YEARS 18 AND BEYOND.
ARMY LIFE.

At 18 years old I was conscripted into the army for 3 months military training and reserves for a further 3 or 5 years, doing night and weekend training. This was mandatory for all 18-year-old youths. Some years later rules were changed to the selection on their birth dates. Again, there were more changes to where conscripts served in Vietnam. This had far reaching effects on numerous diggers. Now there is no conscription, I believe a return to some form of it would change the youth from boys and girls to men and women. My

18 and in the army

training was at Puckapunyal in 15th Battalion signals. There were some so called "soldiers" that had never been away from their mothers. They couldn't clean their boots or wash and iron their clothes. Some would cry half the night for their mummy. This type of life I was used to. On many occasions I along with other self-reliant diggers had to teach these people a bit about being 18. I would help once only, after that they were on their own.

After discharge from Puckapunyal, the next few years were spent at 4 Div Signals in South Melbourne doing night parades, weekend training and 2-week bivouacs near Puckapunyal called site 17.

On discharge I could have received Service Medals. For reasons I can't remember, I didn't apply for them. In recent years I applied and was presented with them in my own home by MP Mr Bob Baldwin. (See photo). Not many if any would have been presented medals in this fashion. Bob and his secretary took photos and stayed for morning tea praising Beryl's cooking. Little did they know it was a date loaf packet cake. Generally, home cooked goodies were the order of the day, but we had just returned from a trip, hence the packet cake.

Receiving medals from MP Bob Balwyn   Life in Puckapunyal 1957

BREAKDOWN AND OUR FIRST HOME

The pressure of life was too much for me and got to me in 1957 resulting with me having a break down. My girlfriend at the time, Evelyn Hutton, and her mother, took me in. They had a flat in Chaucer St Moonee Ponds. The back veranda was converted in to a sleepout where I stayed until Evelyn, and I got married on June 13th, 1959. We continued to stay there until we purchased our own home in 1960. We purchased in the northern out skirts in the suburb of Glenroy. At this point other exciting things happened, our first son Gregory James was born on 7/10/1960. Not as exciting as becoming a father but another first was the purchase of my first car, a 1948 Ford Prefect. I paid one hundred pounds ($200) for it and sadly it was a disaster. I knew little to nothing about motor cars and was ripped off. After a couple of years of holding it in 2nd gear and stopping every 150 Kms to tighten the fan, I sold it for twenty-five pounds ($50) without a battery.

      Glenroy was a new but poor area. There were no roads, no sewerage (nightman once a week) no telephone, no streetlights, no public transport, and few neighbours. The nearest shops and public transport were about one mile away over mud and slush. We needed a car, and the Prefect filled the void for a while until I purchased a 1952 humpback Vanguard for one hundred and fifteen pounds ($230). Again, that did the job for quite a few years until it died. Both cars taught me a fair bit, engines, gear boxes, differentials, carbies, breaks and clutches were pulled down and restored until such time they became un-fixable.

We had a made road at our front but needed to travel over unmade conditions to get in and out. The reason for our made road was that our house was on a new sub-division but in the middle of unmade streets. Purchasing on a made road allowed us to obtain an extra two hundred and fifty pounds ($500) from the Fawkner and District Co-operative Housing Society to their maximum lending of three thousand pounds ($6000). The sewerage and made roads took until 1969/70 to eventuate. Until then all waste and storm water ran out to the streets. The pong at times was fairly strong with wash up, washing and kitchen waste sitting in gutters waiting for a good rain to wash it and the residue of dirty nappies away.

Primitive and unhealthy it may have been, but I was determined not to waste money on rent. In finding this house, naturally we looked at others. I was railroaded into signing a contract for another place with my block of land as security at 400 pounds ($800). The thieving B***** had me sign something totally different. I immediately sold the block from underneath him for six hundred pounds ($1200) and took off to my solicitor.

After telling him my woes he gave me the biggest lecture for signing something that I was not familiar with. During the lecture he said to me "how old are you". I told him that I was almost 21. That's it he said, you're under 21, forget about it, I will sort it out. I never heard another word from the cheating B*****.

Our home was a simple 3 bedroom brand new weather board of about 10 squares. There were no paths or garage. The price was four thousand one hundred pounds. ($8200). I had sold my block of land for $1200. A loan from the Fawkner District Co-op for three thousand pounds ($6000) left me five hundred pounds ($1000) short. I took a second mortgage at exorbitant interest rates. As earlier stated, "I wasn't going to rent and throw money down the chute." This meant I had to find more money as my wage could not sustain my outgoings. I took on any and everything, gardening, mowing lawns, washing down houses and working as much overtime as possible. I later developed a lawn mowing round of about 12 customers earning enough to balance the books. Our first son was born on 7/10/1960 as previously stated meaning everything was done on one wage. Our second son, Darryl Andrew, was born on 6/5/1963 and daughter Annette Joy was born on 28/5/1966. The three children were all born at Vaucluse hospital in Moreland Melbourne.

All the hard ships were eventually put behind us. I firmly believe that a strict budget plan taken out with the Credit Union made the difference between success and failure, having a house of our own or losing the lot.

Along the way I built an extension on the rear of the Glenroy home as a rumpus room. I didn't have modern tools such as electric saws and drills. I also dug the sewerage trench by hand to a depth between 50 cms to 2 meters deep and 20 meters long, built a garage and put down a lot of concrete. All this was done by hand and by me.

Around 1975 we decided to sell our Glenroy property and purchase in the leafy suburb of Greensborough to start a fresh beginning as the Football club was taking effect on our marriage. We purchased a 4-bedroom brick veneer with two bathrooms, lounge, dining room and rumpus. The Glenroy home was on the market for $38500 which was top dollar for the area. The Glenroy sale almost came to fisticuffs when the Agent tried to talk me into accepting $31500 whilst rubbishing my extension and handy work after telling me that it would sell in a minute for $38000. I gave him 30 seconds to leave the property before I would either knock him out or throw him out and not to return. His boss came back to me with $36500 providing I left the above ground swimming pool. The deal was done and dusted without further fuss.

FOOTBALL. EDFL.

After my stint at Carlton, I joined Moonee Valley in the Essendon District Football League in 1958, staying for eight years then going on to coach them in 1965. I played mainly in defence, preferably at full back. I was a dour defender giving nothing away, playing it hard but just inside the rules. I was never reported. My ability to kick a drop kick to the centre of many of the suburban grounds made it a fair choice for playing me at full back. My coaching rules were different to what the "Valley" players were used to. I was not prepared to waste time and effort to finish in the bottom half of the premiership ladder. I tried to change their mentality by adopting "no train, no play". I also tried to abolish their Friday card and booze nights.

Duck opening day was more important to a few of the players than their Club and the Saturday game as several decided to attend the duck opening and leave the team short of players. Another incident that should have warned me that the job in front of me was going to be hard was during pre-season training. I had mapped out a street course of about six Kms which included Maribyrnong Road hill. A tram rattled by me and surprise, surprise, there seated were some of the players enjoying a free ride up the hill and nearer to the club house. So much for trying to put miles in their legs.

All these instances and more were non-negotiable, so I had to go at seasons end.

One door shuts and another one opens.

Ascot Youth Centre (AYC) approached me to coach them in 1966, straight after getting the sack from Moonee Valley. AYC had been struggling for years. I took the job and coached them to Grand Champion Premiers.

(Undefeated for the year). My second year with them was not as rewarding. We were put into a higher division and did not cut the mustard. Players had left after gaining their dream in 1966.

AYC amalgamated with Riverside Stars in 1968. Amalgamating was necessary in the area as there were too many teams and players were hard to find. Four or five clubs in the inner suburbs were affected. Some amalgamating and others disappearing all together

I had two years with AYC prior to their amalgamation with Riverside Stars. The travelling time and cost was not worth it, so I hung up my boots. For winning the Grand Final in 1966 I was paid their complete bank funds at the end of the 1966 season. Twenty-five dollars was their total. This equates to less than one dollar per week. The experience was tremendous, it taught me a lot about myself, leadership, people management and confidence which I took into my working career to my advantage. Whilst the $25 was all they had, the side benefits more than made up. Through this, I believe my employment advancement was greatly improved. Thanks to AYC.

Bad luck Moonee Valley, it was your call to give me the flick.

THE 1966 PREMIERSHIP

The 1966 season became famous in the Essendon District League as AYC proved that a team/club could go through the entire year un-defeated. It wasn't easy but with discipline and sacrifices it was obtained.

The Club recruited well, the surprising thing was players wanted to return and see for themselves what this new coach could bring to the table. The season was plain sailing until the finals started.

The 2nd semi-final, we played Essendon High School resulting with a "cliff hanger" result. We won the game by a few points with injuries galore. In the last quarter I packed the back line with fit players and left the forward line to do their best. If Essendon High had not kicked 2 goals 8 behinds in the last quarter the premiership would not have been AYCs. Injuries would have caused a possible walk over if we had to turn up for the Preliminary Final the following week. As it was with the weeks break, we still had some suspect players. During the week off, the majority of "cripples" passed their fitness tests. Trevor Fitzpatrick, our number one ruckman, had a very bad ankle sprain. On the Thursday prior, he had to pass his test. He was successful but told me much later that the pain was almost too much to bear but he wanted to play on grand final day.

Fitzy was picked in the ruck on the Thursday night so everything seemed OK. On the Saturday Ken Pridham, one of our better players, came to me with a knee injury incurred at work and wanted to pull out. He was strapped and asked to do his best. Not only did he do his best, but he was also awarded Best on Ground. Also, un-be-known to me, Fitzy was still hobbling and had cooked up a plan to send Hopey, our centre half forward, into the ruck whilst he played at full forward. Martin Herron took the centre half forward spot and change rucked with Hopey. I was at full back and couldn't do anything about it until quarter time, I was furious.

Airport West, our opponents were off to a good start leading by 3 goals with in the first ten minutes. I was the culprit to one of the goals as I was caught holding the ball after a savage tackle that left me very groggy. Number 16, one of their better players was the player that slung me to the ground. Shortly after it was my turn to square the ledger. I gave him my best hip and shoulder with my knee catching him in the ribs and chest. He was carried off and finished for the day.

Their Captain/Coach took himself off at ¾ time. At that stage, scores were forty odd points each and we were kicking into a strong wind. My instructions were, attack up the middle, forget about the wind and to run, run, run. The replacement for their captain/coach was a first-class idiot. The first thing he did was to give me a kick under the chin when the ball was up in our forward line. Later we were defending in the goal square, I was scrambling on hands and knees when he gave me two rabbit killer punches, I was waiting for a free kick but play- on was the umpire's call. Finally, I got a free kick and within seconds we goaled. From there on we ran away to a reasonable win.

After the game I asked Grubby, the umpire, about the two rabbit killer punches. He said, "It was always going to be a free kick to you, but I wanted to see how much you could take". Thanks, Grubby.

Back to Fitzy and Hopey, it became one of the "best selection decisions ever". Hopey did well in the ruck and Fitzy kicked 2 or 3 goals on one leg. As for number 16, he evened up the score the following year when he got me a real beauty in the ribs resulting in 3 cracked ribs and out for a month. I would call that a fair result, but we won the Grand Final.

Chapter 6

LIFE AFTER PLAYING
HADFIELD F.C. FORMATION and LATER.

At the conclusion of my coaching in 1967 in the EDFL, the Hadfield Youth Club Football Club heard of my coaching ability. In 1969 Leon Coventry approached me to coach the coaches as they were high on enthusiasm but low on ability. At the same time, I coached the under 15s until the end of the season due to their coach having a bad accident. The following year I coached the under 11s under the Youth Club management with very ordinary results. I was also elected President of the football section of the Youth Club. The Youth Club set up was not a good model, Leon and I decided that a break away from it was the best option. We took this idea to the football section of the Youth Club and their main body. Discussions and meetings took place with Broadmeadows Council and the Youth Club. After negotiations for equipment were agreed to, the Youth Club gave us their approval to go it alone. A meeting of interested locals was held to form a committee of the Hadfield Football Club in 1970/71. I was elected their inaugural President and Leon their secretary. This was a great honour to me, and I would think Leon would have had similar feelings. It was now time to find a league for both juniors and seniors and a ground to play on. We had been using the Hadfield High School paddock when governed by the Youth Club. This was not suitable for our needs going forward with the introduction of an open age team. We were allocated Reddish Reserve by council. Again, a primitive piece of ground with stones and thistles. Working bees and hard work by the council and the committee readied the ground to basics for the beginning of the 1971 season. The juniors would keep playing in the Northern Districts. (NDFL) so that much was easy. The seniors were to be formed and become the backbone of the Hadfield Football Club. We approached the Essendon District Football League (EDFL) for entry. I was well known by their hierarchy of McTaggart and Marcy from my AYC days, and we were duly accepted into the EDFL "C grade" competition for 1971. During this time, we had to write a constitution, find players, make some money, select colours, we decided on Hawthorn's as they were not used by teams in either league. These were some of the tasks but there were many.

We adopted the Hawthorn team song and emblem. (The hawk). It was a frantic time but to be part of the foundation of a suburban culture was something to cherish.

I was also involved with the Carlton Little League team. At half time of the main game, the Little League kids would entertain the crowd as well as themselves. They thought it was the thrill of their young lives to be decked out in the colours of their league teams. I had the job of umpiring a match at Carlton against a Hawthorn team. I awarded a free kick against a Carlton player for holding the ball. It so happened that the free kick was awarded directly in front of the Carlton grandstand. At that moment I thought I had started World War3. I was abused, yelled at, and called various names and it was for a scratch match between under 11 kids. I immediately

Umpiring Little League

knew what the real league umpires endured week after week. A great experience for me and the players concerned.

In the beginning Hadfield fielded 4 underage sides in the NDFL. Under 11s, 13s, 15s, 17s and one open age side in the EDFL competition. I coached the under 11s and won the premiership in our first year beating St Albans, a local church side and red hot favoritest at North Melbourne's AFL ground.

1st team to win, a flag for Hadfield. U11 1971

This was to be the first premiership and milestone for the Hadfield Football Club, justifying our bold move.

The little kids were the foundation stones of things to come.
It was also a wonderful day in my life and the sporting lives of my 20 little players furthering the establishment of The Hadfield Football Club. As time went on, some of this team went on to play in the seniors and some stood for various club positions. I can still remember the number of under 11s at training in our first year. Some evenings there would be close to 100, some as young as 5 or 6. To keep enthusiasm up I would pick the side to play that week's competition match. For the rest I would pick two sides, give them a coloured band each and play an intra club game. Some of the little ones would get muddy to show mum and dad that footy was "really tough and rugged". Two little brothers about 5 and 6 years of age were picked on opposing sides, I placed them on the wing,

They ran out onto the ground holding hands, almost immediately they sat down and made daisy chains while watching the ball go over their heads. If they were picked, they were happy and so were their mums and dads. This is what made the club so special to families and retained the interest of the kids.

A couple of weeks later our Seniors defeated West Coburg in the "C" grade grand final held on the Keilor ground. Our number one ruckman, Ron Waugh went down with an illness during the preceding week of the grand final. Lively debate at selection took place on his replacement. I wanted Graeme Berry; a player overlooked on many occasions as he was not in the clique. In the end I got my way, Graeme rucked all day to near exhaustion. He was best on ground, thank goodness, justifying my arguments to have him included in the side

Hadfield Seniors Premiers 1971

This gave Hadfield two premierships in our first year. A tremendous achievement for a newly formed club. This showed further justification in our desire to form The Hadfield Football Club. I continued the Presidentship for 6 years making it 7 after the Youth Club stint, I also continued with coaching juniors.

I coached an under 13s and an under 15s to further premierships after the under 11s and a runner up under 13s. The under 13s win was a surprise to everyone as we defeated the short-priced favourites, Thomastown by 4 points on the Coburg ground.

Hadfield Under 15s Premiership 1977

The under 15s win was a super win. It rained all the prior night, and the ground was very wet and heavy. Our opponents were East Coburg, un-defeated for the year. They had defeated us by 20 odd goals at our first meeting of the year, 12 on our second and 6 in the semi-final. I had thoughts of the best way to defeat them. I sat the team in front of a black board each training night drilling the boys in what I wanted. I believed we needed continuous movement of our on-ball players to confuse the opposition coach and players. This would allow us to drop someone into the centre to relieve our best player to drop back to the half back line. He got leather poisoning from marking and gathering kicks. Their coach couldn't find a way to counter our many moves. At times our players also got confused. I can remember one of our rovers yelling out to me "Mr Fox where do I go now". I was always called Mr Fox, an early teaching of respect and discipline.

I must mention half time. We were in the sheds when our back pocket player yelled out "we can win this". He was an ordinary player; his name escapes me. I was looking for an inspiration from somewhere to hammer into the minds of my players. His words were just what I was looking for. I demanded all players to take his belief, confidence, and enthusiasm from him by going to him and touching him reaping his feelings from him and instilling his feelings into themselves. This was magic, all in the room swamped him, including players, coach, and spectators, touching and shouting **"yes, yes we can win this."** This was the stroke of a genius. We hit the ground full of confidence and went on to win. A lot came from that ordinary player's six super words **"yes, yes we can win this"**.

These words, the rain and the 5 unattached umpires, 2 goal, 2 boundary and the central all had some impact on the result. The five umpires making sure their rough and dirty play did not occur. This no doubt affected them as they liked to go the man, the punch, and the rough stuff. In our first encounter I wanted to remove our boys from the field due to their bash tactics, it was blatant thuggery. With the 5 umpires supressing their dirty tactics, we won quite easily. Their coach was devastated and wanted to know how we beat them. I told him that we were the better side with a much better discipline and a better coach. That went down like a lead balloon.

That win made a total of four premierships in my coaching career three with Hadfield and one with AYC in 1986. **Not bad ah.**

LIFE MEMBERSHIP

During my Presidential reign I was awarded the first life membership of the club. Johnny Walker, our treasure was awarded the second. Maybe it was too early in the life of the club for such awards, but the members deemed plenty had been achieved and the

Number 1 Life M/ship Medal

foundation of club rituals, culture and history had to start somewhere. To say the least I was stoked to receive such recognition.

A women's committee was set up to supply canteen goodies to visitors and our local mums and dads. The first canteen was in a tent erected each match day. The ladies worked out of the tent for about a season before the Council built us a canteen on the end of the club house. Things were primitive but a strong bond and desire to achieve made for a successful beginning. Joy Walker was recognised sometime later and awarded the first ladies life membership medal. She was a tireless worker with the club and in the EDFL as a club delegate.

DISCIPLINE.

A show of strength prevailed early in the life of the club. We had a couple of troublemakers. They were often grizzling about what we the committee had decided but rarely did they come to us for ratification of their gripe. On this issue we stood a very good player down on disciplinary grounds. The trouble being that he was in with the troublemaker's clique. In their wisdom and without coming to the committee, the players went on strike just prior to the match against Brunswick City. We the committee did not back down, that would have ruined what we were trying to instil. **Discipline.** We decided that we would find some shorts etc and strip with some juniors and a few loyal seniors and take to the field. Of course, we were well beaten but Brunswick City treated us with respect and no injuries. I remember being late home half boozed, but the message given was all worthwhile. Most of the players apologised for their foolishness and returned to the fold. The couple of renegades accepted but never changed. They were a constant pain in the arse.

Two other incidents come to mind;

Number 1.

We held a dance at the local school hall, a couple of members didn't see eye to eye. A couple of biffs and all hell broke out. I summoned committeemen to help regain order. This was duly done as we threw out the offenders. When going home I noticed my car had been damaged. The culprit was found in the following days and was brought to my house for his punishment. An under 17s player was the guilty one.

A phone call to his father was made, his father arrived and hit the roof. He disciplined his son by making him pay for his indiscretion. ($350). What was done in private was not leaked, we never had further trouble from him.

Number 2.

After a home match a "playing hero" of the Club removed his jumper and struck the umpire. He thought if his number couldn't be taken, he would get away with his despicable act. Before he had left the field, I had collected his clothes and met him at the door. I threw his clothes at him and ordered him off the premises. The club drove the umpire to hospital and generally looked after him. We suspended our guilty player for 10 years which was ratified by the league. This action saved the Hadfield Club from untold repercussions and hefty fines.

It could have spelt the end to the Hadfield Football Club if the above action was not taken. The juniors would not have been affected as they played in a different league.

Can you imagine the repercussions if the committee of the day didn't see through the bluff that senior players placed as more important than their club. Day after day the committee had to wrestle with tough decisions with some risk attached to their own welfare. Tough we may have been but honest we were. The club still stands because of discipline and strength.

STEPPING DOWN

With all the heart aches and drama, I loved that club and worked my butt off for it, but you can only take so much.

At the AGM when I announced my retirement/resignation from the Presidentship I turned my back on those present and said, "You can now remove your knives". I noticed the troublemakers squirm and slide down in their seats. The others gave me a spontaneous ovation.

I retired from office in1978/9 after moving from the district to Greensborough in 1976. A few years later,1979/80 I think, I was asked to coach the open age 2nd 18 side which I accepted. It didn't sit well with me being the coach of the left-over players. I suppose I was number one or nothing. After the one year I retired for good concentrating more on our new home and work, moving up the ladder of opportunity. A great deal happened in the next few years. One thing was my permanent move inter-state to NSW in the Xmas of 1997.

In 2011 I returned from NSW to Hadfield's 40th anniversary, donating my club blazer back which is now permanently on show in their club rooms.

As I write this story it is my desire to get to their 50th year Celebration Ball, on July 10th, 2021, at Essendon Fields Hyatt Hotel Ball Room.

Foot note. The Covid 19 virus has altered everything. The Ball has been postponed twice. Who knows it could be postponed indefinitely? By the time my story is completed I may be able to give an up-date.

See page 112 for up-date and fiasco

EASTER AND THE EASTER BUNNY.

In the 1970s we placed a caravan on site in a caravan park at McCrae on the Mornington Peninsula. A lot of golf was played at Century Park Rosebud and Cape Schank. An inter caravan park competition was a highlight each year with a night out at the Century Park club house for all participants and families where winners and losers could brag or sulk.

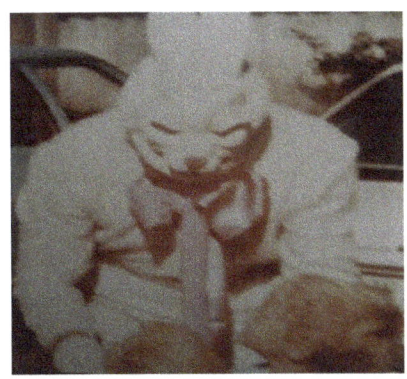

Easter Bunny. Who is it?

At Easter I would dress up as Easter Bunny giving Easter eggs to all the kids in our park. To avoid recognition, I would leave the park, get changed and re-enter through the front gate with my basket of eggs. No one knew that I was the Easter Bunny.

Next to our van was little Robert with his single mum and his grand-parents. He got all dressed up in his suit and waited at their annex door for the bunny to arrive. When the bunny finally arrived at his van, he had tears rolling down his cheeks and crying with excitement. He took his egg and was so thankful it brought tears to the Easter Bunny's eyes. We had a game of bunny hops prior to moving on to the other kids and then leaving the park.

On my return sometime later, young Robert came running up to me and said "where have you been, you have missed the Easter Bunny". He told me all about the happy day in his young life when the Easter Bunny paid him a visit.

Not many if any knew who the bunny was. To sit through his story of when the Easter Bunny paid him a visit, along with seeing this little boy's face and his excitement was worth all the sweat lost in the Easter Bunny suit.

Our Greensborough home.

MARRIAGE FAILURE.

The football club took a lot of time and money, I believe it affected our marriage as things started going pear shape. It was thought that the shift from 47 David St Glenroy to 157 Plenty River Drive Greensborough may save the day. We bought a brand new 4-bedroom brick veneer home with 2 bathrooms complete with rumpus room. This put us back in debt but wages were a lot better at this point in time.

Whilst the shift righted the ship to some extent, the chasm was getting wider. When the children began work and becoming independent the glue began to weaken. I was advancing in my employment and Evelyn was working at a Catholic school on office duties. I could see us drifting apart, communications were getting less and less, my work hours were getting longer and longer. It was my call; I had had enough. I shifted out to a room in North Melbourne before finding a flat in Fairfield.

Separation was followed by divorce proceeding and the splitting of belongings. This was reasonably amical, and I paid Evelyn what the court handed down. By way of a loan from the Credit Union I was able to buy the property back and Evelyn was able to buy a property in Watsonia. I was back in bigger debt again.

It was a difficult time in my life and no doubt it was also difficult for Evelyn. Thinking that the children would be able to accept things, I was proven wrong. I tried to keep in contact with the children, Greg was in the army, Darryl was with K Mart and Annette was with Telecom, a position I was instrumental in her obtaining.

I was not received all that well by the children in fact I was shunned. In time the two boys accepted me back into their lives, but Annette did not, no matter how much I tried. I was not invited to her wedding which will be touched on later.

SUSIE, WHISKY AND PUG THE DOGS.

After our divorce I bought the house back as mentioned prior, there were" *some bits and pieces, which I "inherited*" such as the outstanding mortgage and Susie the dog.

We always had a dog, there was Whisky who drowned in the pool. He would walk along the fence top and along the pool edge. He must have slipped in during the day and swam until exhausted. He ripped the lining to pieces before drowning. He was called Whisky after drinking whisky given to him by a neighbour, becoming horribly drunk. Annette, my daughter, wanted a replacement. We went to a kennel in Wonga Park. There were plenty to choose from. They were lined up along the fence barking, yapping, "look at me, look at me, please pick me".

There was another one away from the fence line looking very lonely and sad. Annette said, "I'll have that one," so the replacement was done. She had been named Susie with the black patch. We named her Black-Eyed Susie. Her heritage was various, mainly Foxy/Blue Healer cross.

She became my constant companion, I was ever so grateful that she was left behind. On arriving home from work each day she would not let me enter the house before she had told me all about her day, barking, yapping, snuggling, and dancing with her tail wagging profusely. She would not enter the house without being coaxed. She was taught that from an early age. On cold nights I would coax her in and spread a sheet in front of the heater in the rumpus room where she would snuggle down until she got too hot, then she would drag the sheet across the room to a cooler corner. She was almost human.

A trip up to the farm would make her week. She would make friends wherever we stopped. On one occasion she be-friended a bus load of pensioners, enjoying a day trip and held me and their coach driver up with all of them wanting a pat and a talk.

Somehow, she knew when a farm trip was on, she would wait until the car boot was open and dive in burrowing down as far as possible. No way was she going to miss her trip. At times I would have to unload the boot to get her out placing her in the front seat. She was now happy knowing full well that the trip included her.

After Beryl and I were married, Susie became Beryl's walking mate. They would go for an afternoon stroll around the neighbourhood or to the park. Often, due to her age, she would renege and lie down. Beryl would tether her to a tree then go home and get either the car or the wheelbarrow to take her home.

On her last trip to the farm, she went up the hill and lay down in a hollow. All the cows gathered around her bellowing. I think it was the animal's way of saying goodbye to her. They knew she was very sick, and her death was imminent. I went up and carried her home as at that stage she could not walk. I took her to the vet next morning knowing it was the end for her. Her life ended after **Nineteen years less 6 days.**
I took her home and buried her in the fernery complete with a monument containing her lead, collar, and plastic squeaker bone. Yes, I cried and was not one bit ashamed. She was my best friend in a lonely part of my life.

Prior to Susie and Whisky, we had a Pug. Puggy by name, an ugly little fella, but very cute. Unfortunately, he was hit by a motor bike when meeting the kids after school. A trip to the vet with one eye hanging out. The vet stitched it back in but it popped when the stiches were removed. His eye was subsequently removed. A year or two later he was again meeting the kids after school when a car on his blind side struck and killed him.

BERYL

Through my work I met a woman from Sydney, Beryl Woodward. We courted for 4 years commuting between the two cities by way of overnight coach trips.

Beryl Woodward

The bus left Melbourne at 7pm arriving Sydney at 7.30am. On the way, there were 2 comfort stops, the first at Albury and the second at Goulburn. In the winter Goulburn's temperature would be minus 4 or 5 degrees. Not the best breakfast stops at 3 or 4am. Why not fly you may ask; I could hardly afford the $25 bus fare let alone contemplate plane travel. In 1990 on September1st we were married. More of that later.

The Woodward family & Spouses
L-R. Beryl, Neville, Gloria, Lyall, Edith, Bill, Nancy, Malcom, Sue, Ken, Di, Ron.

They are very *close-knit* family. They were all born locally and have returned to Taree and Forster to retire except for Ken and Sue who live in Grafton. We all spend time together wining, dining, and enjoying each other's company.

Chapter 7

EMPLOYMENT

As previously stated, I started with the PMG on 25.1.1954 as a technician- in-training. Before that I worked at the Castlemaine Post Officer as a JPO for 2 months mainly delivering telegrams. The training was over 5 years. After successfully completing the 5th year I was entitled to sit for the Senior Technicians exam to start my advancement up the promotional ladder. It took me 3 or 4 attempts before success. A senior tech was equivalent to a leading hand or foreman. As stated early I chose Exchange Installation as my discipline. This entailed the building of equipment into telephone exchanges to convert the manual system into the first stage of automation. Geelong had the first automatic exchange in Australia. It was commissioned in July 1912 and referred to as the "X" exchange. After we built and tested the new automatic exchange, we would cut it over from the Magneto or Common Battery system to the automatic system which responded to the rotary dial driving electro-magnetic switches to make the connection. People had difficulties dialling their own wanted numbers instead of a telephonist saying, "number please" and connecting them by cords. It was a brand-new experience connecting yourself to someone miles away.

Electromagnetic equipment. Ivanhoe Exch & Mario Doville

We would, at times, modify or add to the existing equipment. This was a good job as you moved from exchange to exchange, never bored by sameness. I worked mainly in northern and western suburbs of Melbourne progressing up the ladder of opportunity from technician to Senior technician of various levels to Supervising Technical Officer (STO) which put me in control of an exchange or area employing 20 to 40 staff. I then gained Principal Technical Officer grade 1 (PTO1) status in charge of bigger and more complex projects. My first station as a PTO was Russell St exchange and city area. A big modification at Russell, employing 50 plus staff, 8 or 10 at Batman/City West, and a few at Civic. A short time later Exhibition was to come online with the latest technology of our time. Fully computerised, more challenges. When Exhibition came online, I oversaw the closures of Russell and Civic with both exchanges and subscribers being cut over to Exhibition. Not long into this phase I was promoted to a PTO2 position as the Installation Managers 2IC Southern Area Melbourne. This area was from St Kilda to Mordialloc across to Springvale, Caufield and back into the city. This was one third (1/3) of the Melbourne metro area. My office was on the 5th floor in 31 Spring St Melbourne.

A huge restructure in about 1984 saw me obtain a promotion to Installation Manager South. This incorporated a large increase of the original Melbourne Metro area, taking over the outer fringes of Melbourne and the tip of the country area. It also saw the technical people replace the University graduated Engineers with direct line control of staff and projects This didn't go down too well with some engineers.

Mal Evans my Material Officer

My area stretched from St Kilda, following the beach to Portsea, the Hastings peninsular, Tooradin, Narre Warren, Belgrave area, Springvale, Ferntree Gully, the Dandenong Hills, Richmond and back into the city It was a huge area with about forty exchanges employing over 300 field and six office-based staff. As this was a new area, staff were obtained from the existing Metro East area and the Country area. Other managers found this was their opportunity to unload problem staff. I can tell you, not knowing a lot of the staff, I drew the short straw on many occasions. The Country transferees were not happy having to join Metro management. At the end of the day, we were able to achieve what was necessary to have a solid and respected group of dedicated staff. It was challenging to say the least but with four field "lieutenants" we conquered what I thought was the impossible.

After another restructure in 1992 I was Acting Branch Manager looking after all of Melbourne Metro areas and all Tasmania. Over 1200 staff with 25 to 30 direct reports. It is acknowledged that seven to ten reports are the normal. The introduction of a Queensland Divisional Manager saw my need to request early retirement. The stress was leading me to an early grave. I had done my time and duly left after near on 40 years, saving my health and sanity. I had obtained advice from a Financial Adviser that with my superannuation and redundancy I was very able to retire. The last few months had become an un-manageable and un-healthy environment. On the 25th of May 1994 I had my retirement function attended by approximately 100 people at the Hawthorn Football Club. More on retirement later.

TOTAL QUALITY MANAGEMENT

My boss at that time was Bill Goudie, a wonderful man who would encourage you to stretch and make your own mark. He introduced Total Quality Management (TQM) into our Branch, Network, Design *& Construct* Melb. TQM is virtually bottom-up initiatives being investigated, streamlined and adopted where and if warranted. Through TQM our Branch won an award of excellence defeating Toyota, BHP and others. We were presented with the award by Victoria Premier, Joan Kirner at a lavish dinner where all participators were in attendance. This was a wonderful achievement and envied by many in Telstra and numerous in private enterprise. Bill Goudie was a legend. He died at an early age but left an indelible imprint on me. It is my belief that Bill's push to make our Branch stand out was the catalyst to us winning the award. He took his entire management team to Mannum, South Aust. where we were stretched out of our comfort zone. Such activities as abseiling down a mine shaft, crossing a gorge on a rope some 50 metres above ground. Pretty frightening stuff but it moulded us into a very formidable management unit. Spur of the moment exposure to decision making is one example. At a dinner during the course, I was thrust into the MC position of a concert without notice or content until the last minute. The effort put in by individuals was rated by a judging panel.

The team building throughout the many activities, both practical and theory, was nothing short of a brilliant learning curve. In short it was an initiative to trust and back your colleagues together with "bottom-up management". It is surprising what can be achieved if the rank and file are listened to and their ideas are discussed, accepted, refined, and adopted. At the completion of our adventure our Branch members would "practically kill" for each other such was the camaraderie and trust we had developed.

At the outset I categorically stated that I was not interested in this "waste of time exercise". I'm so grateful I was virtually told "you're going, full stop". The experience and learning of this venture helped throughout my management and later life years. Thanks Bill, for your confidence in me. You were a legend and great leader.

THROUGH THE BILL GOUDIE ERA

Through the Bill Goudie era many evening dinners took place after a hard day's work on programming, scheduling, planning and the likes. On occasions, to give a light-hearted atmosphere after our hard day, he would ask me to give a talk on some make- believe topic. I think Bill respected me and my humour.

On one occasion Bill had just returned from TQM studies in America with Dr Demming the guru of the subject. He had taken his TQM understudy with him- A WOMAN. That gave me the perfect lead in to give a big rubbishing. The whole of our management team joined in. It was an off the cuff talk. Bill enjoyed it along with the group. It went over quite well. No harm done and respect still intact.

On another occasion I had an inkling that I would be asked again to give a humorous talk. I went prepared with a poem referring to retirement as some were nearing that time. It's called:

"The Telecom Reunion"

We used to meet at places like this
To chew the fat and get on the p*** (grog).
To study the budget and the years works.
To listen to patter from informative jerks.

We had world best practices and TQM,
A shift in culture for Construction men.
There were graphs and charts, weights and measures,
All the jargon to ruffle our feathers

There, stood Goudie "tall" and proud
Head and shoulders above the crowd.
With doctrine from Dr Demming USA,
Bill was known to have last say.

He took his team to South Australia,
Dressed us up in Rambo regalia.
Over the side and down on a rope,
There wasn't much time to think and mope.
BRM conquered his fear,
JB was a pain in the rear.

EC plan was the management tool,
The system we all tried to fool.

We had Carry-In and Carry Out,
Among the things to report about.

Lines, cut overs and 2 meg streams
Are now distant memories in our dreams.
It's now golf and bowls, caravanning too?
All the great things we've got time to do.

So, thanks to the team that made it worthwhile,
All different in status, rank and file.
We gave our best to Telecom Australia.
Are the shares we purchased a monumental failure
Forget that now and any other delusion,
Just enjoy this Telecom Reunion.

In my office discussing a TQM initiative with Bill Goudie (left),
Doug Campbell (Aust Chief of Engineering) and my working party

Rat, Cat and Dog Jargon.

At a high- level meeting, chaired by Ron Dick, Chief Supervising Engineer, a couple of highly educated engineers started on the big word, look at me syndrome. I got jack of this and interrupted stating "Knock off this tripe and talk so everyone can be in the conversation". One said to me; "What do you mean". True, this was my reply; You would say "My canine is chasing a feline which is going to devour a rodent". I and the majority would say "My dog is chasing a cat which is going to eat a rat". After great applause from all including Ron Dick, I was known as the Rat, Cat and Dog man.

RIGHTA

Another amusing encounter was at an end of year meeting with my section and the hierarchy of the branch. I was congratulating the troops for doing lots of good things for the completed year and outlined some good achievements as well as some failures.

I said, "We did **alright,** but we will have to do it **"righta next year".** Well, the word "righta" became the word of the year. A simple mistake with a lot of meaning.

It's a bit like the KISS principle. *"Keep it simple stupid"*.

LIFE AFTER

Another restructure saw me advance to Acting Branch Manager of Melbourne Metro and all Tasmania, a staff of 1200 plus. This was a ridiculous situation with over 25 direct reports. To manage properly, 7 direct reports is about the mark. This situation gave no time for man management and planning as reports and hitting budgets took all my working time plus half the night.

A heated discussion / argument with my boss (everyone has to answer to someone) paved the way for me to seek redundancy and leave the organisation after 40 years.

I retired too early but the redundancy payout, long service and superannuation meant I could manage providing I didn't go mad and overspend. This turned out to be the right decision as the pressure I was under was beyond my capabilities and most likely would have been beyond every bodies. If I had stayed on in that type of environment, it is doubtful if I was to make old bones.

To compensate my early retirement, I purchased a small office cleaning business. I had clients in the Footscray fruit market, North Melbourne, Collingwood, Kew, and Greensborough.

The business generated funds to allow Beryl and me to build a lovely home in Forster NSW. We are situated on a hill overlooking a bird haven, water glimpses and the golf club which is 400 meters down the hill and 500 meters to One Mile Beach. It is paradise and will do until my demise.

Retirement

My retirement function was held at the Hawthorn Football Club Social Club. A massive turn up of my staff, numerous retired colleagues, friends from within Telstra, friends from outside, my two sons and wife Beryl.

Strangely my immediate boss did not bother, sending a representative. You would think I was worthy of his presence after nigh on 40 years' service. Poor form I thought. Nevertheless, a great send-off was organised for me. It was the done thing to take up a collection in the proceeding weeks. This was done and a huge amount was collected for me to buy a new set of golf clubs. My organiser, Mal Evans did a wonderful job right down to me buying drinks from the collection. His only problem was that he forgot to put a limit on the amount across the bar. At the finish I did not have sufficient to buy my gift. I put in the short fall and used the set of clubs for many years. It was a win /win result.

A hand shake and on your way

Some of the crowd at my retirement

Chapter 8

SPORT.

At school the usual sports were available. I excelled at football, not bad at tennis and squash. Cricket was a dead loss to me. I couldn't bat but could bowl a fair leg break.

I was trying to improve my batting by practicing in our driveway at 6 Forest Street Castlemaine. Graeme, my brother, was bowling and I was attempting the late cut. If I got it right the ball would crash into the hedge between us and the Kaye family. Graeme pitched one a little wider, I square cut it straight over the hedge into Kaye's lounge room via the closed window.

Mrs Kaye was home, so we sheepishly went in to explain and retrieve our cricket ball. She took some time to answer our knock, when she did, she was shaking like a leaf. She told us that the refrigerator had blown up and was scared that something further would explode. When we told her that our cricket ball had broken her window, she seemed relieved. We found our ball under the lounge. She said that Gordon, (Mr Kaye), would be home soon and to explain it to him. This we duly did, his reply to two kids improving their cricket shots was, "You will have to pay for it". Over the next month or two we paid a little each week until we had paid him one pound ten shillings. ($3). What ever happened to house insurance and be nice to your neighbours?

GOLF.

As I got older golf was the sport that I fared reasonably well at. My brother introduced me to golf at the Yarra Bend Golf Course and I can remember my first game. After waiting in a queue for a couple of hours we moved onto the first tee. There would have been one hundred waiting for their turn. While waiting in line there was always comment on the swing, stance, follow through etc of the people on the tee. When I stepped up, I knew people were saying all of the above about me. I hit the ball, thank goodness, but it went only a few yards to the right and under a bush. I kicked it behind the bush to be hidden from the "experts". Finally, I got onto the green and wheeled my buggy straight over it. This is not allowed as I found out from my brother and others in my group, telling me in no uncertain manner to walk around the green, not over it.

My Hole in One

On the Yarra Bend course I had my only hole in one. My work mates and I would play golf on our rostered day off. On this particular day it rained and none of the boys turned up. I joined up with a stranger from Northcote. On playing a par 3 of 90 odd meters, I hit a nine iron **and in it went**. I did hand stands in my excitement. My playing companion said "Good shot" as he hurried from the Tee.

Ready for an API event.

Good shot, it was a bloody ripper. As we were on a public course playing social golf it was not recognised by anyone, **except friends.**

I took my score card to work on the Monday to show and be congratulated by my friends. Their response was flattening.

"Anyone can put a one on their card". So, my only ever hole in one was not worth tuppence.

RIVERVIEW, LATROBE and API

I must have improved over time as I joined Riverview (Ivanhoe) representing them in pennant matches. Later I joined La Trobe, a private club on the Yarra flats in Fairfield. I played off single figures for 3 or 4 weeks (9) then drifted out to between 12 and 14.

During my early years in the PMG /Telecom I joined API (Aust Post-Tel Institute.) This was a wonderful organisation catering for lots of activities with sport being a major one. I was right into the golf side of things, participating in golf weeks and inter branch tournaments. I was successful at Bairnsdale, one of my early golf weeks, winning the weeks first prize in my division. I won it with a putt of about five meters on the 3rd play- off hole. By the time I had finished telling of my win, the putt had grown to "at least fifteen meters" and probably still growing.

I was elected to the API Board in 1986, serving up until my retirement in 1994. Again, this was another learning curve. I worked mainly to improve member participation in holiday housing and sport, mainly golf.

Our Branch, Exchange Installation, was successful in 1993 winning gold medals in the final at The Peninsula Golf Club for beating some 20 Branches in the inter-branch knock out competition. This competition was spread over several months and played all over Victoria. In 1994 we were not as fortunate winning silver under similar circumstances, when the final was played at Cobram/Barooga Golf Club.

Gold Medal Winners

Gold Medal 1993

THE FORSTER GOLF CLUB and MELBOURNE CUP DAY

On shifting to Forster, NSW I joined Forster/Tuncurry golf club. The club has two courses 7 Kms apart. One in Forster and one in Tuncurry. They are very different like chalk and cheese. Tuncurry is a sand belt type course rated in the top 100 courses in all NSW. Forster is a bit rougher but is Head Quarters with a lovely club house. Tuncurry is having a new club house built, thanks to a government grant. It is due to open any minute. My handicap as I write this is 20 a lot different to the nine, I reached when I was about 45 years old. Still 20 and walking 18 holes twice a week is not all that bad at 84 years old.

MELBOURNE CUP DAY.

We are so fortunate to live so close to our club. It provides good meals, friends and entertainment in a lovely setting and environment. We try and use their facilities as often as possible. Beryl and I always book for Melbourne Cup Day. About 400 people book in for lunch and enjoy a lot of fun. Beryl has won the best hat and best dressed sections on different occasions. We won the best dressed couple, going as owners. The sweeps and famous "wooden horse cup "are highlights. On one occasion I won the famous wooden horse Cup/raffle

As owners and the winners of best dressed couple.

collecting over $1100. The cup/raffle is almost impossible to win. Firstly, you buy a $5 raffle ticket, after all tickets are sold six (6) winning tickets are drawn out. These six now draw a horse number from one to six. I drew number 4.

A dice is thrown and if the number relates to your horse, that person takes one step forward. This continues until someone crosses the finish line and is declared the winner. The winner takes all the raffle money after all bets are paid out. There is betting with odds. I was 8 to1 and a few people backed me As I said "it's hard to win" or maybe just luck.

VETS

The golf club has a veteran's club within the main body. To join you need to be over 55 and hold a playing membership with the main club. I was elected to the Vets Committee as Vice President and the Travel Officer positions and received life membership for my years of service and effort. I started the overnight as well as one day trips. These trips were to selected clubs within about two hours travel time. I always hired a bus/coach to enable all participants to have a few ales without the worry of DUI chargers.

The overnight trips were a real joy. That's the best way of explaining them without getting some travellers in hot water. One such story should be told and I'm sure the late Kevin Drew would not mind. The trip was to stay overnight at the Kurrie Kurrie Hotel/Motel after a game at the Muree course in Raymond Terrace on our way down to the Kurrie Kurrie course. The accommodation was three to a room. The publican treated us like royalty with a good evening meal and copious amounts of alcohol. The late Kevin Drew and the publican overindulged on red wine, drinking to all hours. Naturally, Kev went to bed a little worse for wear. At some stage during the night Kev had to have a toilet visit. Kev always stated that he tripped and fell hitting his head on a bed leg. Blood teemed from his self-inflicted injury soaking his pillow and sheets. Next morning the publican was up bright and early preparing our breakfast of bacon and eggs. Kev not looking too good apologised to the publican for the mess. Apology accepted was the publican's call. Kev struggled through some breakfast to ready himself for the Kurrie course. It must be said that Kev completed the round with a very bad score, got on the coach and fell asleep. He always stated that it was one of the best trips ever arranged although he missed a fair bit of it. This was agreed to by many.

Both day and overnight trips were booked out very quickly. To fill the bus was the easiest part of it, controlling the boys was sometimes not so easy. I received many accolades for organising such wonderful times from people looking for something different. To this day, the trips are still recognised as one of the best things in the Vets club.

Politics within the Vets Club took its toll on me causing my resignation. I have lost my keenness but continue to support them in a very different way. My resignation saw a lot of trippers give the Vets away and trips are not what they used to be. A shame.

I accept the fact that every thing has a used by date but a bit of effort by a couple of golfers could have kept the trips going. It is often said to me that the trips are sadly missed. Once events like this lose momentum they just die.

Winning a major Vet trophy 2009

Vets Xmas party with John McLeod

The Jones perpetual trophy presentation. Presented by Mrs Noreen Jones

Perce Drury accepts his trophy from Capt John MacLeod

Nev Fox, John McLeod presents to Allan McCarthy

At a Vets Xmas I dressed up as Santa Claus distributing gifts of lollies to the Vets members. This went over very well but has not continued. To me fun like this should be carried on, it makes "old men" cherish the moment.

Chapter 9
THE FORSTER CUP and SAUCER TORMENTS

Another series of trips I arranged and organised were for fellow golfing mates and their wives. These trips were associated with the API, (Australian Post Tel Institute) of which I am still a member. API run a golf 3day weekend event. We would tag on to the tail or organise to go prior to their weekend.

The Cup and Saucer Perpetual Trophies

Our "tournament" was played over a total of 5 rounds spanned over 7 to 9 days. Each day players were scored points depending their position in our field. If there were 8 players the winner would receive 8 points and last would get 1 point. At the conclusion of our "holiday" the player with the most points would receive the FORSTER CUP for men. The ladies were calculated the same way with the winner receiving the FORSTER SAUCER. Hence the name of our event was "THE FORSTER CUP AND SAUCER CHAMPIONSHIP." The cup was a mounted insert golf hole cup with flag and the saucer was a silver tray with a small broach of a lady golfer attached by way of super glue. Roy Lawford was the maker and donor of both. Going with winners there must be losers. Coming last daily incurred a stupid doll, the weakest link, a sword or knife to put yourself out of your misery or something befitting their effort. Coming last over the entire tournament meant something much more fitting. One year at Parkes it was called the Booby Prize. Roy Lawford had the distinction of winning it, an old bra donated by Beryl and padded out, had Booby printed on the right and Prize on the left cup. Roy had to parade in his trophy for the night. As he was parading a chap walked by, stopped and returned to see if what he saw was for real. He wandered off shaking his head, probably wondering if he had stumbled on a pack of queers. Over about 14 years we visited Coffs Harbour, South West Rocks, Parkes, Wellington, Wangi Wangi, Toronto, Goulburn, Gundagai, Mudgee, Cessnock and Coota- bloody- mundra. Wellington, Parkes and Mudgee were visited more than once. Each venue had their own stories which were many. They ceased when we all got older (ancient) or people went to God.

You can talk to any of the Cup & Saucer mob about these trips, but be prepared to be entertained for some time with stories of the presentations and the novelties given away each day. On most trips, we all stayed in a caravan park in our own vans or in cabins. Evening meals were always together where the drinks would flow along with Banta and Bull S***. Yes, we loved the week away with some of the best people you could possibly find. These people still reminisce over the great times and great memories of times now gone bye.

COOTA-BLOODY-MUNDRA

I must tell one story about our trip to Gundagai. For our last day we had to play at Cootamundra due to Gundagai greens being renovated. The trip was about 70 Kms each way. On arrival at Cootamundra, we asked about the course. We were told that there was only one hill. Sure, there was only one hill but you had to walk around and around it for the entire game. Hence the name **Coota-bloody-mundra.**

Nev Livingstone (playing off 14) was having a shocker hitting into fields of rocks, yelling "Go on get in there" etc. On the last green Nev had a 10-to-12-foot putt. How could you possibly do it, **he completely missed the ball.** Naturally a special trophy had to be found. A quick visit to a toy shop to buy a knife to slash his wrists with. They did not sell plastic knives for safety reasons but allowed me to purchase an 18inch long sword. This was presented to Nev. to stab himself in his broken heart.

This is the person that made all the trips possible. The work and detail to make sure everyone enjoyed the week was time consuming and tedious. How do I know? It was me the author of this read. I enjoyed the challenges.

Fun and Frivolity

These photos illustrate the fun and frivolity that went on every day and every year for over 10 years.

Each presentation had its own twist. If you couldn't cop the banter of Kath and Kim, the weakest link, the various dolls and trinkets, the week wasn't for you.

Will it ever return, no I don't think so. Age, ability, health, and death has seen the last of the Forster Cup and Saucer Championship. That's life, we just have to move on and except what is, is.

Nev gets the Dummy.   *Livo, Betty and Ron their with booby prizes.*   *Beryl gets a doll*

Kath & Kim with "Big Ron   *Kath & Kim with little Cathy*

Nev with Livo winning the   *Alan, Lyall & Vic in discussion*   *Norm and that tie*
dunces of all dunces prize
An assortment of Dunce of the day prizes. Note Kath and Kim.

The group at Wellington.

These photos illustrate the fun and frivolity that went on every day and every year for over 10 years.

BOWLS

I took up lawn bowls at about 70 years old. Four of us started together and later formed a pennant side in the 7s competition. The 1s are the best so you can reason that we weren't that good. We won a few games over two seasons. The team was Lyall Woodward (my brother- in- law), John Hemmingway, my next- door neighbour, Mark McNally a golfing friend and me. I am still playing, making a comeback after the last 3 years recovering from knee replacements x 2, fractured pelvis, seven broken ribs and punctured lungs. I will most likely stay with lawn bowls as my golf is deteriorating at a very fast rate. Presently I play once a week at Forster Bowling Club. I very much doubt if bowls will surpass Golf. Time will tell.

Chapter 10

VOLUNTEERING

On shifting to Forster and joining the Golf Club in was apparent that little or no effort was made to look after gardens. They were in very poor shape. In fact, the presentation of the club was suffering from bad management and lack of funds. At about this time the gate was swinging shut toward total closure. The Club was near broke.

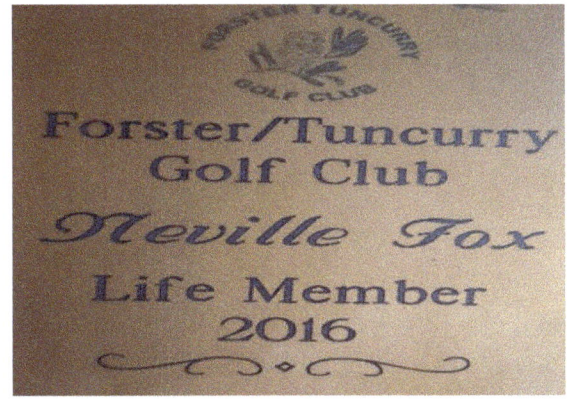

I with 4 or 5 friends started on the garden behind the 2nd green. Months later and numerous trips to the tip with loads of Pennywort the area was sieved to rid any small Pennywort roots and that garden was re-established. From there on many more improvements were made. As the volunteers diminished, brother- in law, Ron Woodward kept helping for over 10 years. Perce Drury came on board after Ron left. On the way David Olliff, Bruce Fisher, Don Richardson had stints of over 5 years. Perce, at 85 years old, and Bruce have retired after Perce put in about 16 years. I have almost retired having a couple of special projects to complete. On their completion I will have given 24 years voluntary service. At 83 I've done my fair share. Perce and I received recognition by way of Life membership. Me in 2016 and Perce in 2018. A very distinctive recognition as neither of us held office. To our disappointment no one has come forward to replace us, all that work on the gardens and now they are deteriorating fast. **Disappointing!**

FENCING

I was asked by the GM Chris Turner to fix or replace 4 fence panels in Strand Street. The 4 panels developed into a major transformation with 4 panels becoming 165. I instigated, planned, purchased, and employed to replace/repair all boundary fence panels in Strand Street. I had help from 4 or 5 playing members but Dirk Diepeveen must get special mention. He is a social member and loves the club and I love his help. With the removal of 26 trees, supply of material and cost of contractors, I have spent nearly $50,000 of golf club money. The club now looks fantastic, attracting more members, visitors, and customers. If the outside appearance is not looking attractive people will not see the inside, **lost custom.**

After the Strand St effort Dirk and I continued fixing all fences, fixing all safety screens, and designing and installing safety nets.

Completed fence at 6th Tee

16th Tee

Driving posts with pile driver. Strand St

Strand St fence construction

MEET and GREETERS

The other request by Chris was for me to form a group from the Vets and man the front door on raffle nights and Sundays. I did the training and roster for the group. Over the next 10 to 12 years about 25 participated in this chore. This was forced to cease due to Covid19 with the club having to employ staff 24/7. I along with the majority enjoyed this chore as it gave us a chance to meet and greet Club members and visitors. We hope it will return at some stage.

LIFE MEMBERSHIPS

One thing to be proud of. Through my life in sport and Clubmanship I have gained recognition of the highest standard. You can't obtain three life memberships from vastly different persuasions unless you give your all. I believe I have done that to every thing throughout my eighty four years. A lesson for any one that cares to read my story is to put in and help no matter what the cause.

Chapter 11

RE-UNIONS

Reunion Number 1

In 1983 The Fox Clan re-union committee, chaired and researched by Beverly Schellen from S.A. organised a reunion for all living descendants of John and Elizabeth Fox, married 1817. I was fortunate to be on the steering committee contributing to the significant day and picking up valuable family history. The reunion was held in Victory Park Castlemaine on a Saturday and Sunday, during November 1983.

My father Harry with L-R Neville, Margaret & Doris   *Edwin's offspring's. Approx 300*

Victory Park Castlemaine. The venue of the 1983 re-union.

There were people from all over Australia. One family from Coffs Harbour, wrote a song specially for the occasion "Let's Make it Back to Castlemaine" (see attached). This was played to death during the weekend. About 350 attended. The furthest was a lady from Western Australia "

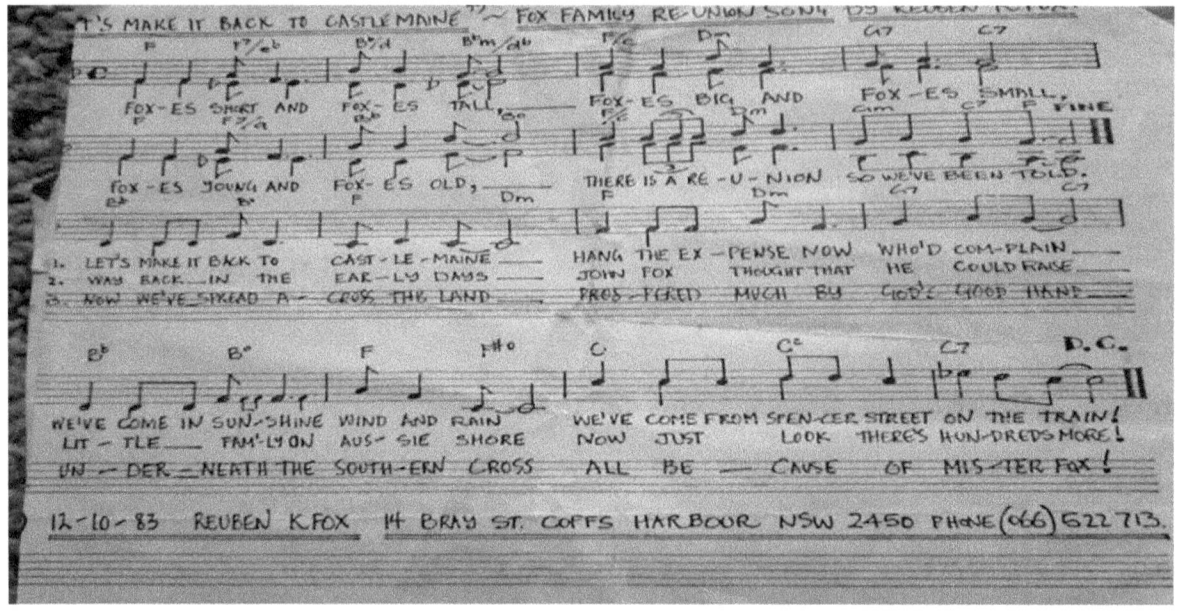

"Let's Make it Back to Castlemaine" by Ruben Fox from Coffs Harbour.

The Mayor, Jack Merlo, welcomed us back to Castlemaine. Thompson's Foundry brass band played on Sunday afternoon. Relics of the past era were on show in homes which could have been visited and of course plenty of stories swapped. Photos of each leg of descendants were taken with my great grandfather, Edwin, featuring with the majority. About 300.
Some legs of decendants did not show, one leg had two people in their photo but Edwin's was well represented as can be seen in the photo.

MASTER of CEREMONY'

I was appointed MC for the weekend. A proud moment for me as I had some of my family including my elderly father, Harry, present.
On the Saturday night we gathered in the RSL hall where the song "Let's Make it Back to Castlemaine" was unleashed. It was composed by Reuben K Fox from Coffs Harbour who attended. As the M.C. I had nothing much to offer. I can't sing and was forbidden to tell my jokes (a bit risqué), instead I wrote a poem titled, "The Reunion", which goes some way of telling the Fox story. That was also tabled for the first time and like the song both were played or recited over and over. See page 80 for the two extra verses 4 and 5 incorporating Harry and Edna along with the entire poem.

On the Sunday, dignitaries spoke of the moment and the Fox family from yester year to the present.

Special gifts were given to the youngest, the oldest, and the furthest travelled. The lady from W.A. was a clear winner.

Probably one of our biggest mistakes was not advising the business houses how many were to come. We simply did not know, hence there were shortages of accommodation and food. Everyone managed and hailed it a great success. Special thanks to Beverly for the family trees, hand compiled, and books written. She did a fantastic job from start to finish.

There are two small books on the early history;
1." History and descendants of John Fox of Leeds 1789 – 1983"

2." Fox Family Tree Charts "Both books compiled by Bev Schelling. 196 Kenny Rd. Ponder SA 5288   Ph 08 85692692.

REUNION NUMBER 2

Nephew Wayne Vick (son of Doris) said to me one day when I was visiting his father, Bob, in the Wangaratta hospital.

He said," Unc, why don't you get our family together before it's too late, you are all getting older." Wayne called us "The Fighting Foxes". I thought about it for a while, then decided why not. I sent letters out to get a feel of things. The response appeared to be positive, so the planning started. What Wayne was referring to about being too late had already started. Our sister Margaret Priest had died of cancer some years ago, her family were contacted. Betty Organ, who I believe was the main reason for the family break up, received her invitation but unbeknown to me she was in her last stages of cancer. She died within weeks of receiving my invitation so the make up between us was a non- event. Doris, Graeme, and I went to her funeral which went some way to mending fences. Graeme who was unknowingly caught up in the family collapse was first to reply with a big YES for his entire family. I had arranged for a trip back to our Rushworth farm, to the place of birth for Graeme and me. The present owners were very welcoming. They have turned 362 acres able to milk 70 cows max, to a business milking up to 700 three times a day.

They have acquired many more acres by taking over adjacent properties. Their milk, with two other farms, is transported to Darwin non- stop in giant road tankers to feed the city. They have up to 500 calves at any one time. Their milking plant is a rotary, milking 80 to 90 at a time. The cows are strip fed with not much room to lay down. Things like this are hard to imagine but it is a business of providing milk. A climb through the old house which was in very bad shape brought back lots of memories causing

plenty of discussion. Since our departure in 1948/9 a few mod cons have been added. Naturally a new house together with the rotary milking plant. The thing that caught our eye was the electricity meter at the front door of "our old house" had lots of memories and discussion. Electricity had been connected since our departure. We survived on kerosene lamps, lanterns, and candles.

Doris, Graeme & Neville at the front door
Note the electricity meter and the cobwebs.

The cobwebs were another attraction.

The entrance gate still stands featuring the properties name. "**Kargell Park** and continues to swing on the original concrete posts that my father, Harry, made and carted to the site. The posts are 40cms X 40cms standing 2 meters above the ground and have a stylish top to them. They must have weighed a ton. The gate and posts were erected in about 1945.

The front gate to Kargell Park. L to R, Neville, Graeme and Doris

A welcome by the Mayor, Mr Homes, a relative of a neighbour from years gone by, and a Historian, together with lunch and the tales of the old days helped us re- join the fracture of our family. Today, Doris, Graeme and I are great mates.

A write up in the local paper encouraged some old neighbours and school friends to drop in, a couple did, namely the Stylers and Blacks. All in all, a top day with the result I had set out to achieve, achieved in spades.
I have added two verses to the original poem I wrote for the Castlemaine re-union in1983. The Rushworth re-union contains the two verses to incorporate Harry and Edna, our immediate fore bearers, and I believe this goes a long way to give background and completion to my story of the Fox Clan from 1816 to the present, 2023.

<u>The additional two verses. Verses 4 & 5</u>

The story continues and must be told
Of Harry and Edna and their fives fold
To Rushworth, via Lake Cargelligo, was not planned
But circumstances dictated, with their passion for land
So farming at Rushworth was their last resort
362 acres of prime land was bought
After buying and building Kargell Park
Harry and Edna were making their mark.

With five kids to help with all the jobs
A bloody tough life to make their bob.
Their five kids are ageing and dying out
With Betty and Margaret already gone
Doris, Neville and Graeme are still about
But time waits for no one, it may not be long
So their children's resolve must keep the name strong
To continue "THE FOX FAMILY" on and on.

THE RE-UNION by Neville Fox

November 1816 Elizabeth Clarkson and John Fox were wed.
Thirteen children, one later died, they were to rear.
So, thirteen children had to be fed.
They decided to migrate, which doesn't seem fair.
Leaving five in Leeds, County of York,
Seven to travel to the Adelaide port.

John's death in 1851
Saw Elizabeth and family on the run.
To Horsham Victoria, they were to stay.
Where the boys took to work with horses and dray.
But the rush for gold at Castlemaine

Saw Joseph, Frederick and Edwin leave Horsham to stake their claim.
Carters of dirt, to be washed was their job.
Can you imagine their pay? --- Just a couple of bob.

A future in farming, must have been seen.
For farms they obtained at Strathloddon, Campbells Creek and Yapeen.
To this very day, the Fox name is legend.
In the Castlemaine district, where some of us were bred in.

Times have moved on to this very day.
And we are gathered together pilgrimage way,
To make new acquaintances with lots of lost kin,
So, what better way for us to begin,
Than to embrace each other at this re-union
and pledge to each other, --- A LASTING RE-UNION.

The story continues and must be told.
Of Harry and Edna and their fives fold
To Rushworth, via Lake Cargelligo, was not planned.
But circumstances dictated, with their passion for land.
So, farming at Rushworth was their last resort.
362 acres of prime land was bought.
After buying and building Kargell Park
Harry and Edna were making their mark.

With five kids to help with all the jobs
A bloody tough life to make their bobs.
Their five kids are ageing and dying out.
With Betty and Margaret already gone
Doris, Neville and Graeme are still about.

But time waits for no one, it may not be long.
So, their children's resolve must keep the name strong.
To continue "THE FOX FAMILY" on and on.

Both poems composed by Neville Fox for the Fox family re-unions at Castlemaine on 24/10/1983 and modified to suit the Rushworth re-union of 8/11/2015.

My Immediate Family History

Harry, married Edna Hicks on 27/6/ 1928 (Harry died 26/9/1985)
(Edna died 13/10/1982)
Doris, Married Bob Vick on 27/9/1952   (Bob died 13/9/2020
(Doris died 26/12/2022)
Betty, Married Geoff Organ on 19/ 5/ 1962. (Betty died 20/5/2015)
Margaret, Married Martin Priest on 2/ 5/ 1959. (Margaret died 18/10/2002)
Myself Neville, Married Evelyn Hutton 13/ 6/ 1959. (Divorced 8/9/1986)
And Married Beryl Woodward on 1/ 9 / 1990
Graeme, Married Norma Tetu on 11/ 4/ 1968.

Ancestor grave sites. Castlemaine Cemetry Victoria

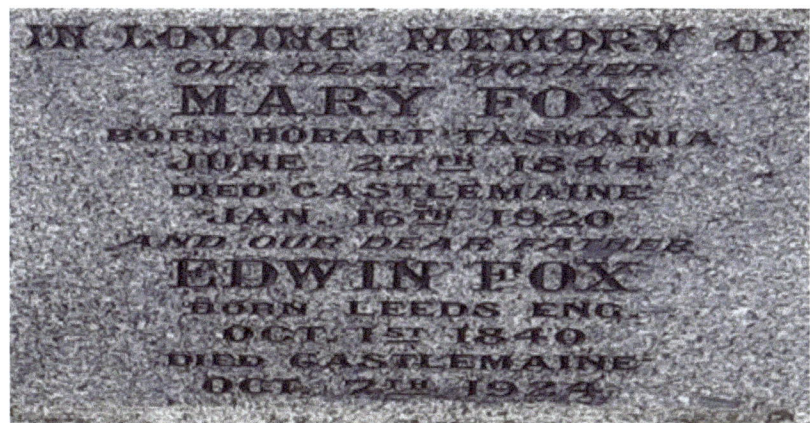

Great Grand parents **Mary and Edwin.**

Grand parents. **Eleanor and John** .

Mother **Edna**

Father **Harry**

All smiles for the family photo at Rushworth Re-union   8/11/2015

BERYL'S FAMILY.

By comparison, Beryl's family is the very opposite to what ours was. I do believe that in their family if one cuts their finger the rest bleed. Their family is one in a million.

Her mother and father have long passed. The six children they reared are all married with their partners still alive. Of the 12 of us, 9 are over 80. The eldest being Ron at 89 and all still going strong.

Beryl is the matriarch of the family making sure all communication lines are open. They wine, dine, visit, and entertain each other on numerous occasions each year. They are a credit to their parents as not many, if any, disputes have occurred to this point in time.

Her family has taught me that there is a different way of doing things, very different to *The Fighting Foxes*.

Chapter 12

WEDDINGS in my Family.

GREGS

My eldest son Gregory James married Elizabeth Carr on 19/5/1984 at Parkville, Melbourne. At the time he was enlisted in the Army. He served six years with no overseas missions. He was stationed for the majority of his time in Canberra as an electrician. He and Elizabeth produced three children, Brendan, Elysha and Nicole. They spent some time living with me after his discharge from the Army. They bought a home in Drysdale (Geelong). After their marriage breakup he shifted back to Melbourne and formed his own business. Greg never re married but had a long relationship (14 years) with Cheryl Heath. He has recently purchased in Townsville close to two of his children, Brendan and Nicole and his grandchildren, Memphis, Bella and Zander. Elysha still resides in Geelong with her son Coulton.

DARRYL'S

Second son Darryl Andrew started his working career in sales. He was good at what he did obtaining "gun salesman" with FAI security. His reward was a world trip. This line of work ended when he lost his licence. A chance of a plumbing labourer job developed into an adult plumbing apprenticeship at 42 years of age. He was dux of his course twice and presented with an award by renowned AFL coach, "Tee shirt" Tommy Hafey.

He married Megan Breen at the Bendigo Cathedral In February 2001. They bought a 10-acre block in Lockwood South (Bendigo) and built a lovely home. This was all lost in a divorce 10 years later. During the marriage, 3 daughters were born, namely McKenzie, Maddison and Analise. In an attempt to save their marriage, they shifted to Sunbury to be closer to work. This had little to no effect, in fact it was a disaster as Darryl lost plenty in the divorce. His girls live with their mother in Moama and see their dad every second weekend, during school breaks and over Xmas. It's not the best set up, but the best provided by the court system.

Darryl shifted into my property at Guildford until it was sold in 2020. (More of that later). He was working as an industrial plumber on high rise buildings in Melbourne for several years. He caught an animal to human virus called Rickettsia. This has resulted in he being unable to work and has been on sick leave for over 12 months. Fortunately, he has a partner in Lisa Foley. Lisa is a nurse at Mornington where they now live. Without Lisa I don't know what would have happened to Darryl. Unfortunately, they have recently gone separate ways. Lisa remains in Mornington and Darryl has relocated to Townsville where he bought his own home.

Hopefully he will return to good health where a new life awaits him.

ANNETTE'S

My only daughter, Annette Joy Fox (McCallum's) wedding day was one of the worst days in my entire life. The reason being, I was not invited. Even though I was not invited, I went to the church with my suit etc in my car in case of a change of heart in the dying minutes. It was a dream I thought may have happened, but not to be. I sat in the rear pew wearing dark glasses to hide the tears. She looked lovely with her two brothers, Greg and Darryl guiding her down the aisle and giving her away. I hung around outside the church standing out like a sore toe. Some guests spoke to me, shaking their heads in disbelief. Photos were taken with me missing out on her great occasion.

A sad, sad day for me.

To this day I still don't know her reasons for barring me from her wedding and life, as her mother had moved on and we were amical in the separation.

ANNETTE AND FAMILY.

Annette and her husband, Dale McCallum purchased and moved to Goornong after a short residence at Bendigo. I tried to visit her there but was told by her Nanna that she was not receiving visitors. Some years further on Beryl and I were invited and accepted to their home in Goornong where we had a BBQ lunch. She and her family had a Xmas with us in Greensborough along with Greg, Darryl, and their families. As time went on, she and Dale had three daughters, Katherine, Carlee, and Alana, to whom I continued to send cards and presents for their birthdays and Xmas. When they moved to Huntly (Bendigo) we would drop in when driving down from Forster to Guildford and Melbourne. To be honest, we were not received at all well by her or her family. In disgust with her rudeness, we ceased visitations. It is about 18 years since any meaningful dialogue has occurred between us. Some terse letters have to and froed over time but nothing to explain the reason it has all end up pear shaped.

MY WEDDINGS.

1959. Wedding 1

My first wedding to Evelyn Hutton on 13/6/1959 does not need to be discussed in detail. It is noted for history. Evelyn moved on and married George Cairns. He died some years ago. Evelyn now lives in Bendigo with her daughter Annette and son in law Dale.

1990. WEDDING NUMBER 2.

Our wedding in Ashfield. 1/9/ 1990

My wedding to Beryl Jean Woodward on 1/9/1990 was a real hoot. Beryl had not married before and had to do all the arranging and organising as I was still working and residing in Melbourne. She arranged her church, Saint John the Baptist C of E in Ashfield NSW for the wedding ceremony.

The Sydney Rowers Club in Five Dock was her choice for the reception and a one-man band for the entertainment and dancing. Her niece Sally Papworth (Maine) was her bridesmaid. My son Darryl was my best man. Darryl and I drove up from Melbourne on the Friday, staying at a motel in Ashfield with my sisters Margaret and Doris along with Melbourne friends. The wedding ceremony was the normal run of the mill, but the reception was a blast. Everyone wanted to make Aunty Beryl's special night something to remember.

After photos and pre dinner drinks, we were wined and dined in style. The music was so great that the dance floor was packed from go to woe. We were having such a fabulous night our departure from the Rowers Club was just prior to close. Darryl picked us up next morning and drove us to the airport for our honeymoon. He then drove my car back to Melbourne. We honeymooned at Townsville and Cairns returning to Sydney and packed up Beryl's unit. We drove her car back to my place in Greensborough where we resided for about eight years prior to retirement and moving to Forster NSW.

Chapter 13

A BIT ABOUT FORSTER

As stated earlier, I am Victoria born, moved to NSW on Boxing Day 1997. After meeting Beryl and becoming engaged, I decided to purchase a block of land in Forster. A friend from the Forster Golf Club suggested I look at the two blocks next to him in Daphne Street. I offered to purchase the two blocks, but the owner would not come down and I would not go up. We met at a compromise for one block at 34 Daphne Street.

Forster is a seaside township with beautiful views from the hills and suburban living from the flats. We are on a steep hill. (See photo).

OUR FORSTER HOME

Whilst in Melbourne I drew plans for our Forster house. What I did one night I would rub out the next.

It was a process that took two years.

Beryl wanted 4 things;
1. Plenty of light.
2. French/Bay windows in the front.
3. A dining room for her entertaining.
4. Rear exit not via the laundry.

After two years and reams of paper I had achieved the impossible, a house plan to suit all criteria. Finally, it was finished, and we were more than happy with the design. Beryl's brother, Malcom, was contracted to build our two- story mansion of four bedrooms, downstairs rumpus room, three toilets and bathrooms, dining room, lounge, kitchen, and double garage underneath. We still

Fairly steep block.

love it after 23 years. We won't be going anywhere soon, health permitting. A lift is in the process of being installed in readiness for older age. Our en-suite has been remodelled to cater for "roll in shower". All is now set for older age.

Forster has everything with hospital, ample shopping, 3 large clubs, 3 bowling clubs, 2 golf courses, surfing, boating, fishing, eating out at the many restaurants. Accommodation is plentiful with about 12 motels, 8 or more caravan parks and numerous high-rise apartments.

Forster and its neighbour, Tuncurry are joined by a 631-meter-long bridge making the area very unique and picturesque. It is well worth the effort to holiday in this piece of tranquillity.

630-meter bridge between Forster and Tuncurry in the background.

Our home at 34 Daphne St Forster

from our balcony

<u>FRIENDS.</u> We have a very good life in Forster with numerous friends from numerous grounds. A lot are from the golf club, Probus, Beryl's church and family/relatives on Beryl's side. We entertain a fair amount with Beryl being a fabulous cook. Each year we put on an Australia Day party for up to thirty friends. It started out being our golfing friends but now has grown to include family and neighbours along

With Max Walsh enjoying a drink.

with golfers. The catering is practically all done by Beryl and me. A couple of the ladies are given small jobs to lighten the load on us. The feast is a traditional Aussie treat, roast lamb and roast veggies, damper, lamingtons, Anzac biscuits, trifle and pavlova with berries and ice-cream. The place is decked out in Aussie flags and guests are expected to dress for the occasion and BYO. Plenty of Aussie music tops off a top afternoon and evening. A charge of about $10 each almost covers the expenses.

Chapter 14

TRAVEL AND HOLIDAYS.

Holidays when the kids were young started in a tent at Rosebud fore shore, Warrnambool fore shore, Inverloch and a couple of other seaside camps prior to the purchase of an old caravan. After using it for a couple of Murry River holidays it was later permanently in a park in McCrae. After selling it some years passed before I purchased another one as told in the caravanning section.

My travels have been many and varied, from overseas by air and sea, interstate by car, air and caravan and intrastate by coach.

Singapore and Hong Kong in 1979 to celebrate 25 years in Telecom, travelling with fellow trainees of the PMG 1954 intake.

China in 2007 with Probus was a great experience. Travelling up the Yangzi was very good but the food was hard to take. The poverty and conditions are extreme compared to the Australian way. We spent 2 weeks sight-seeing and travelling throughout China.

At this point I must digress to explain Probus as the majority of travel has been with the organisation. Probus South Pacific is a worldwide organisation initially formed to cater for Professional and Business people, hence the name, Pro-Bus. Now adays anyone can belong provided you are of good standing. There are many clubs throughout. We here at Forster have 3 or 4, some are men only, women only, or like ours a mix of men and women. We meet monthly where invited speakers, speak on various subjects of interest. In a nut shell it's a friendship club doing what all elderly people like, enjoying life such as the trips mentioned.

New Zealand in 2011 was another trip covering both islands travelling by plane and coach. Another excellent experience.

Coach trip to Mungo National Park via Mildura and Wentworth.

New Guinea in 2014 was by ship from Sydney. A very different trip visiting 4 islands. Each being different but the natives made us very welcome and put on culture shows with their dancing and rituals.

Kangaroo Island South Australia and Murray River in 2016. A fantastic trip, flying to Adelaide, Ferry to and from Kangaroo Island, coach around the Island, Adelaide and SA capped off by River cruise on the Murray from Mannum to Murray Bridge and return.

Throughout our 22 years with Probus, the Club has put on a feast of day trips together with the above.

A FLUKE OF HONESTY

It was 2014, we were heading for a cruise to PNG with our Probus Club. It was anticipated that we might dine on the captain's table. Naturally I had to have suitable attire which required the purchase of a new shirt and tie. My wife, Beryl took me shopping to Stockland at Forster. I had to take my jacket and trousers to make the perfect match. After the purchase the "boss" (wife) instructed me to venture out into the rain and secure my clothes on the back seat of our new Hyundai. I hurried through the rain to the car, unlocking as I hurried along and threw my clothes on the back seat. I had trouble locking the car and gave up preventing getting soaked. After more shopping we headed home for lunch. After lunch I remembered that my clothes were still on the back seat. Downstairs to the garage, opened the car door, to my total amazement there were no clothes. Some scoundrels had stolen my wardrobe. Down to the police station to report the robbery and fill out a few forms and back to Stocklands to complain about the lack of security. As I was giving a fair lashing to security, a chap rolls up stating he had found these clothes in his car. I turned and said, "They're my bloody clothes". After some small talk it was discovered that his car, a Hyundai the same colour and model as ours was three bays from our car. He confessed he did not lock his vehicle hence I was able to open it after I thought I had unlocked it. Naturally I could not lock it. For being honest and returning them I bought he and I a lottery ticket. Not a winner.

The wonder of this story was, it was over three hours from purchase to find, we both ended up at the same time and the same place (security) to put an end to my "stolen" clothes drama.

I returned to the police station embarrassed to the hilt to give the officer the solution to the crime. He looked at me as I was a complete dill. To his credit he didn't lock me up, just a smile. To make matters worse, we never made the Captain's Table, so all for nought.

THE TOP END TRIP.

On 20/5/2002 four mates set off for a trip to the Top End. The 4 were Alan Ingersole, Mark Mc Nally, Lyall Woodward and me (Nev Fox). To start with we bought a Nissan 4-wheel drive, a roof rack and all the things to survive such a trip.

Nev Fox the cook.

L-R Nev Fox, Alan Ingersole Mark McNally Lyall Woodward at the top.

We travelled inland on the way via Roma, Longreach, Mt Isa, Lawn Hill, Mareeba, Weipa, Elliot Falls to Siesta. Whilst there a boat to Thursday Island and Horn Island for one day was of interest. The return trip was coastal for a fair bit of the way travelling via Archers River, Cooktown, Daintree. Port Douglas, Cairns, Townsville, Emerald, Carnarvon Gorge, Dalby, Uralla to home.

This could have been the trip of a lifetime but unfortunately, we no sooner left home and we were back. We left on 20/5/2002 and arrived back on 23/6/2002. 29 days to travel 8000 Kms and spend about $3400 each which included the purchase of the vehicle plus personal spending money. At the end of the trip the vehicle was sold without loss.

Siasia Camp site

I believe a trip like this should take 6 to 8 weeks because there is a lot to see and do. Also, it is a once in a lifetime trip and we didn't do it justice. If you get the opportunity, my advice is **Do It**, but have some pre-arranged time lines and itinerary. Select a leader to make sure all parties are getting a fair go.

Most importantly. Take your time.

CARAVAN TRIPS.

Beryl and I under our own steam have travelled throughout NSW, Qld. Vic, SA, WA and Nth Territory. All these trips were by caravan. The two longest and maybe the best were to Darwin, stopping off at Uluru, Kings Canyon, Kakadu, Litchfield, Alice Springs, MacDonnell Ranges, both East and Western and many more interesting places. We visited most towns and places of interest. One of great interest was Mataranka, 420 Kms south of Darwin. We discovered a hot water creek. We hired noodles to float downstream for 100 meters plus, climb out and do it again. This was so relaxing. They have another in a recreation area about 10 Kms away. It has a hot tub but nowhere as good as the flowing creek. We had tea and a show there and met some of the nicest indigenous people you would ever meet.

The other long one was to Perth via the Nullarbor, chasing the wildflowers, as far up as Geraldton and down to the South along the coast to Busselton, Margaret River, Denmark, Albany, via Mount Barker to Esperance before joining up with the Eyre Highway at Norseman. This trip was about 14,000 Kms.

My one regret is not to have done the "Around Australia trip". We missed out on Broome, but we saw plenty. My travel days are over as I lost my nerve towing the caravan through large cities. All trips were terrific. Of course, not forgetting the other fantastic trips throughout NSW with my golfing mates which has been covered earlier.

You can wear a camera out photographing all the wild flowers. The Wreath flower was the most interesting. It grows in disturbed soil generally on the side of roads in areas to the north of Perth.

It consists of just one plant in the form of a wreath. To find it you need to be patient and cover a lot of kms.

We travelled many kilometers to locate a glimpse of this most lovely Western Australian flower.

We found it between Morawa and Mullewa some 150 Kms East of Geraldton on the side of a dirt road. People had driven over others but there were a couple left for us, thank goodnes.

The Wreath Flower.

This would be the most beautiful and unique flower found on our WA wild flower trip. Hard to find but well worth all the effort.

Some of the wild flowers found in WA

Chapter 15

EIGHTIETH BIRTHDAY PARTIES

The first eightieth birthday party was Beryl's, held at the Forster Golf Club on 11/9/2016. Beryl's nieces wanted to give her a party of some

Entering Beryl's party

description as recognition and thanks for all she had done for the entire family over many years. Beryl is known as the **Matriarch** or the **Supreme Commander** of the Woodward family. Starting from the oldest, Ron, and moving through her other siblings, Lyall, Edith, Malcolm, Ken and flowing down through their strings of off springs. There is an understanding, if something has to be done, "We had better run it past Beryl".

Genni took up the challenge and confided with me. I had plenty of time and took it on as a project of silence. Genni would ring me most Sunday mornings whilst Beryl was at church. Over the next five months we rang and invited about 80 friends and relatives with their

Mix and talk time.

promise not to discuss it with Beryl as this was to be the best kept secret for surprise parties to beat all surprise parties.

People came from all parts of Australia plus one nephew from England. On the weekend there were out of town people hiding so not to spoil my surprise. Beryl thought only a few local relations were meeting us at the Club, was she surprised!!!

Beryl and I had to arrive at 6.30 to give every one time to be ready and organised. When entering the function room, the musician and 80 guests burst into happy birthday, cheers, and whistles. Beryl was taken over with happiness and shock, she shed a tear or two. To keep a secret like this for over 5 months, I had to lie both day and night. After the shock Beryl enjoyed the dancing, dinner, speeches, best wishes and so on. I was forgiven for all my lies and stupid replies over all those 5 long months. I even had to ring various people that Beryl may have had reason to talk to prior to her big night and warn them that it was a surprise party and tell lies, but don't tell Beryl anything.

Beryl's 12 nephews and nieces.

On reflection, she gave it a mark of 95 being surpassed only by our wedding which rated a mark of 100 plus.

PARTY NUMBER 2

Eightieth party number 2 was mine. Held at the golf club where about 80 guests ate drank and got merry. Relatives, family, and friends from Victoria fronted up to see me achieve a milestone along with plenty of locals. I was most grateful for my son Greg and sister Doris, with husband Bob, brother Graeme with wife Norma making the journey. It is about 1100 Kms from Melbourne to Forster. Bob was 90 and Doris 87. A great effort from all the Victorians, especially Bob, Doris and their son Wayne to get them here. My other son Darryl was ill at the time and couldn't make it. A big disappointment to me. Music was played but the best entertainment was the speeches, especially M.C. Graham Burns, my brother- in- law Ron Woodward and his

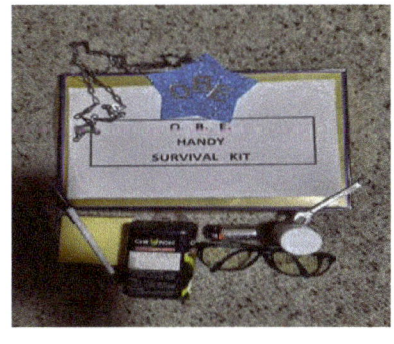

Ron's survival kit

survival kit to see me through my twilight years. Items like batteries, a large one to give me a big boost and a smaller one to give a trickle charge. A note pad and pen to write down what I must remember. Glasses to assist failing eyesight. A spanner to tighten numerous parts including replaced knees and any other moving parts that needs attention. A bottle of pills to control, assist and restore many parts of the body and their functions. A humorous speech very suited to the occasion.

My so called friend Neville Livingstone took me apart on the subject of golf. Talk about humiliation, he had it all. I had to sit through about 20 minutes of it. Fancy criticising me for treading on his line, talking while others are putting or hitting, mucking up the scores, having short drives and many more parts of my game. I need encouragement not humiliation.

The worst complaint was my ability and desire to fart during a game. He never left anything out. My guests were well entertained and so was I. A lot of fun, at my expense, by good mates. I can take it.

Speeches from brother-in-law, the late Bob Vick, son Greg, brother Graeme and work colleague Bernie Millane. Bernie took a different angle, he spoke at length about himself, I don't think I got one mention. Bernie travelled from Melbourne to tell me what I already knew about him. In fairness to Bernie, he was asked by Beryl to speak on my time in Telstra. Maybe he got the wrong message and spoke on his time. All is forgiven Bernie.

An interview by Greg and nephew Wayne on what I think the world will look like in 20 to 50 years hence. An interesting subject. Some classic answers such as travelling to and from work by private plane or drone, similar to the Jetsons back in the 1950/60. All in all, a good night was had and those that could were invited to a BBQ at our place on the Sunday. Beryl was paying so hang the expense. A fair crowd turned up to enjoy BBQ lunch, drinks, and talks. Bernie's speech was highlighted.

Chapter 16

THE GUILDFORD FARM.

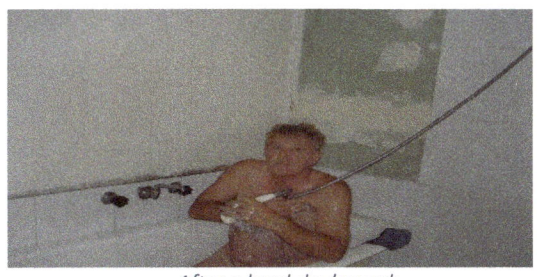
After a hard day's work.

When Harry, my father died in 1985, I with sisters Doris and Margaret inherited the small acreage (60 acres) on Tarilta/ Vaughan Road Guildford. More about the farm is written in the early pages of my story. About 2 years after obtaining it, Doris wanted out. Margaret and I bought her share and continued on. We sunk a bore and ran a sprinkler system to spray water on about 10 acres in the view to growing our own stock feed. This worked to a degree but needed constant watch. The bore cost about $15,000 turning out to be a good investment. The bore went down nearly 300 feet, water was found at 150 feet but both quantity and quality were very poor. The borer suggested that he would supply the manpower if we purchased the pipe for a second attempt. We struck

I hate painting.

plenty of almost pure water at around the 300 feet mark. The Dept of Health certified it suitable for human consumption. We were able to supply the house and stock with a plentiful supply instead of relying on tanks that had seen better days. Harry had installed second hand tanks daubed with concrete both inside and out. If it wasn't for the bore new tanks were needed that would not have been anywhere as functional. We raised beef cattle, teaching ourselves as we went along.

Margie lived in Castlemaine, and I was in Greensborough Melbourne. We also had Margie's daughter Debbie living on the property. This made our venture workable to a point. I had to do a lot of travelling to keep up my end of the bargain.

When Debbie moved out in 1992, Margie also wanted out of our partnership. It left me with huge decisions. Do I buy her out or do I sell? I was already deep in debt from my marriage failure. I was able to borrow more from my Credit Co-op, so I made the decision to buy her out. People said that I was mad, I would go broke, but this land was family history and I wanted to give it my best shot even though I might go down in a big heap. On acquiring the farm outright, I had to paint the house as my intention was to rent it out as a side interest to raise some much-needed money. With some help from friends, I was able to neaten it up and install my first renter,

All jacked up and nowhere to go.

Nipper Lowrie, in June 1993. His rent wasn't that much but was giving me an income, which was badly needed. He fed my stock and generally looked after the place. He stayed on until January 2005. I then put people in paying more and was able to build up my farm account. Eventually big renovations were needed. First was a restumping, as I thought. The floor sloped toward the outer perimeter of the house and sagged in places. I needed a re-stumper, I found one in Melbourne who was prepared to stay on site until the job was completed. He jacked the house up, pulled out the old stumps and said, "I can't go on with the job, the house is full of white ants." Now what do I do? I looked locally and found a young builder in Castlemaine by the name of Josh Butcher. He could not give me a firm quote as he didn't know where and when he would beat the white ants. I trusted him and we got stuck into a major renovation. If I knew then what it was to cost me, I should have pushed it over or burnt it to the ground, but I needed a house on the property in case I had to sell. The land itself was not worth a lot so the house stayed. Although in poor condition it was a sellable property. The cost of the renovations, painting and floor coverings was $42,000. I think Josh Butcher let me off with a little bit as he understood I was in some financial trouble. In 2007 my son Darryl put a new roof on as leaks were further damaging the interior It felt and looked like I was chasing my tail but determined I was to make a go of it. I had gone too far to throw in the towel. To gain more income I agreed to agist my neighbour's cattle. This saved me from trying to farm my own cattle from Melbourne. After Darryl's marriage broke down, he lived in the house whilst working in Melbourne. He started work at 7am in Melbourne. After driving almost 130 Kms to work and 130 home, it was a long day for him. However, during this time, he painted the interior, built, and installed a new kitchen converting the old stove and fireplace into a feature. The travelling was getting the better of him, but the pay was too good to

Darryl's new kitchen and remodelled fireplace.

work local. After an analysis between us to sell or not to sell, we agreed sell was the smart thing to do even though he loved the life in Guildford and I was to lose what I had fought for over many, many years. Darryl was in the Fire brigade, had lots of friends and loved the Gilly. (The old Pub). Due to the circumstances the farm had to go. It had been in the Fox family for 147 years. A hill on the property and on maps is called "Fox's Hill". This was a big deal to me and my granddaughters, they said **"this place is history."** From that you can imagine the agonising thought process and decision that I had to make. It's now a thing of the past. The price was good, and we all got something out of it in the end. We have moved on although it was a tough call. I am probably much better off as I have one less worry and some money in the bank. As has been said before, "One door shuts and another one opens".

The Gilly (Guildford) Pub.

A little bit about Guildford. Guildford is a simple little settlement about 130 Kms from Melbourne, situated between Bendigo and Ballarat with a population of 333. There are no big stores just a pub, a corner store/milk bar, the fire brigade, a hall, and a cricket ground. Majority of residence use Castlemaine or Daylesford for their day-to-day shopping and services. In its day it had lots of pubs, shops, and gold was mined. When the gold ran out so did the population. Now grazing and cropping is the main industry.

A very large gum tree about 100 meters from the store, is where Burke and Wills camped under during their expedition in 1860/61.

The Guildford Plateau is unique as it is a large flat hill. It is referred to as an upside-down landscape surrounding the hamlet, Loddon River, and river flats. It is a pretty little place particularly in the winter and spring. There was an article in the Bendigo Advertiser stating that if you wanted to hear quiet, Guildford is the place to hear it. I witnessed it one Sunday late afternoon when I was sitting on a rock in a paddock watching my stock grazing. It was that still and quiet I could hear their teeth grinding from 100 meters. It was just so beautiful and calming.

Aerial and treasured snaps of the 147 years the Fox family-owned farm situated at 108 Vaughan/Tarilta Road Guildford.
 I have many more if anyone is interested.

The old house at 108 Vaughan/Tarilta Rd Guildford

Dam and Paddocks   **Ready for work**

Overlooking the house from "Fox's Hill" with the Loddon River and Plateau in the background.

Aerial Photos for the Sale of my Guildford Property

THE SALE AND MORE

In 2019 I engaged Cantwell Realestate Castlemaine to sell the property I had used them for many years as my rent collector and naturally they should get first go at selling. For some reason they could not get me a sale. Later I found out that the sales person of my property was concentrating else where. Enough said on that subject. I reduced the price and still no luck. Finally, I took it off the market and was going to change to another agent. This was not necessary as a knock on the door by a woman wanting to buy. She gave a good offer which Darryl had to run past me. No sooner had she left there was another knock. Two gentlemen from Cairns were eager to throw their hat into the ring. Their patter was simple. "We are prepared to pay X dollars no haggling or mucking around". To our amazement they were $25 K up on the lady's bid. We felt obliged to negotiate with the first bid and see if she was prepared to match or better the second figure. It was evidently too much for her and the deal with the Cairns people was done and dusted. A huge price to what I had paid all those years ago when people said that I would go broke.

Whilst the farm was on the market, I decided we should have a wake to celebrate the 147 years of the Fox's ownership of 108 Tarilta Road Guildford. My immediate family of Greg and Darryl plus sons of Doris and Graeme with some of their families along with Debbie, Margaret's daughter attended. After general inspections were carried out, I gave a talk on the history of the place together with a viewing of the five titles that constituted the property. After a hearty lunch and more stories, it was time to say goodbye to 147 years of ownership. All that was left to do was wait for a buyer. This did not take too much longer, and the rest is history.

Part of the families at the Wake

WATTLE and DAUB.

The wake was held in front of the old dairy as can be seen in the photograph. The dairy is unique as it is "wattle and daub" which was quite common way back in the early 1900s. This one is stringy bark saplings, in place of wattle. The saplings generally stood up, side by side and were then covered in mud, daubed, to a thickness of 20 to 30cms. When the daub had dried it was painted with kalsomine paint, a water- based paint. You would be very lucky to find another wattle and daub building as these were not classed as anything of note, until they were all reduced to rubble or fell down with age.

It is also noted that nails, bolts or metal plates were not used in the frames of any buildings. All securing was done by wire twitching. A loop of Number 8 or 10 doubled fencing wire was wrapped around the junction of the two or three timbers, generally wattle, but in our case, it was stringy bark. To tension the wire, a metal spike would be inserted in the loop and twisted around the other end of the wires. By twisting until very tight and just prior to the wire breaking, a very tight and secure joint was made. This art has died out like many others over time. Nails were used to attach the corrugated sheets which were used extensively in that era.

Wattle (stringy bark) and Daub dairy.

NUMBER 1 WINDFALL.

I never offered and was never asked to pay commission to the sacked agent although I was told that he could have requested some payment.
It was unfortunate it came down to this situation. The agent had been with me for many, many years collecting the various rents. I was quite keen for them to

sell for me but after dozens of "lookers" there was not one bid. This was over about 6 months. It was told to me that the effort put in by the agent was a sounding board for other property on the market. Of course, this can't be proved but how strange was it that once off the market buyers come a running and eager to pay the top dollar price.

WINDFALL NUMBER 2.

Another windfall came later when a windstorm knocked a tree over taking with it the front veranda. Just what was needed after the recent sale. I was able to get the insurance company on the go quite quickly. The quote came back at $17,000. I took the money deciding we could re-build well inside the $17,000 and have it done quickly. Darryl was able to get his girlfriend's father to do the job. He lives in Somerville on the Mornington Peninsula, about 3 hours away. Thankfully he accepted. Darryl bought all brand- new material required for $2500. The builder did not want payment. I had to pay, at least the petrol, the answer was still no. At the end I was able to get his bank details and transferred $3000 to him. CHEAP.

All in all, the two windfalls netted me close to $30,000 (The agent's fees and insurance). Add on to that the $25,000 second offer totalling close to $56K above 1st offer. A big thanks to Darryl for his negotiation and building skills.

CLEAN UP & MY FALL

After 147 years you can imagine the amount of junk and litter around the place. It was part of the conditions of sale that the property had to be cleaned up.

Beryl and I travelled down from Forster NSW for the big clean up expecting to stay many days.

I lasted 3 hours on the job when a large and heavy coil of old fencing wire had to be moved to the scrap heap. It escaped me, downhill with our vehicles directly in line. Running alongside of it, I tried to knock it over. The speed of the coil hastened and so did I. At top speed, for a man 80 years old, I was tripped being sent air borne heading for disaster. I

The Killer Coil of Wire

couldn't land on my artificial knees, somehow, I landed on my left shoulder. I think it was the Fox Roll that I invented for the occasion. Down I went like a bag of ????.

On hitting the ground, I witnessed the death tunnel with the bright light way down the end. Evidently it was not my time to meet my maker, being refused entry to wherever. By the same token it was quite eerie and frightened the "bejesus" out of me.

Darryl was in the garage and heard the commotion and rushed to my aid. The language was pretty ripe as I ordered him to get me up so I could continue the clean- up. One effort to stand me was enough. More screams and bad language and he said," What about we get an ambulance". Forty minutes later after lying in the sun with Beryl shading me and keeping flies at bay, the ambos arrived. I had to be pumped up from the ground, then onto a stretcher and finally into the ambulance. With lights and sirens on, we were off to The Bendigo Base Hospital some 60 Kms away. Beryl travelling front seat with the driver and me in the back with the other ambo being fed the morphine stick.

THANK GOD FOR THE GREEN STICK.

Xray's showed seven (7) broken ribs under my left shoulder blade and torn lungs. The doctors and nursing staff were concerned that I could develop pneumonia which could have been the end of me. Seven days in the intensive care unit and a further seven in the ward indicates the severity of my accident. This was the end of my clean up mission. I lasted about three hours.

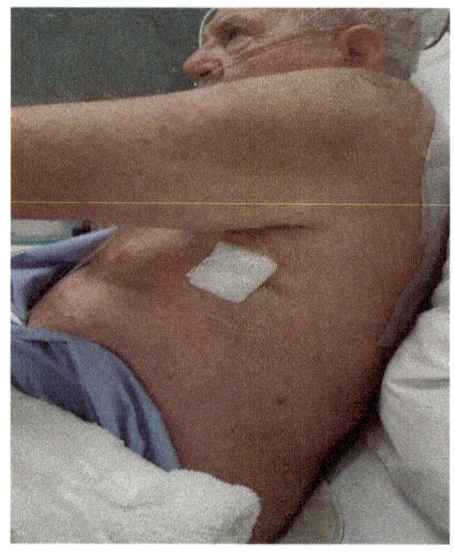

Where the drainpipe entered my lungs.

The only people we knew in Bendigo were the Martins and thank goodness for them. With their care, love and attention we were able to overcome our housing problem for Beryl.

So, it is a special thanks to Helen and Ian Martin for taking Beryl in and allowing me to stay for 3 or 4 days after my hospital release. Following my stay with the Martins, Beryl drove me to my brother Graeme's home in Templestowe for further convalescence before the long trip home to Forster. I must admit there were times throughout my ordeal when I thought I had taken my last breath.

The last 3 years have been very unkind to me;

    2018 I had 2 knees replaced.

    2019 I suffered a fractured pelvis after falling off the 11th tee at Forster Golf Club. I was not drunk, it was 10am and I was playing in the Vets 9-hole event.

What really happened was simple. My new knees were still unsteady from the operation, as I stepped up to the Tee I over balanced falling backwards, I tried to right myself but there was nothing to grab onto, hence I landed on the path, bum first and the rest is history. I got myself home, somehow. I needed a crutch to aid my shuffle, I selected a hair broom from the cupboard and Beryl took me to the doctor. On entry to the doctors, Libby the receptionist said, amid laughter from the waiting room "I've worked here for 25 years and never seen a broom used as a crutch". I had the last laugh as I went straight in to see the doctor in front of those waiting. I can tell you; it was bloody painful.

    Finally, 6/3/2020 I suffered the broken ribs and lung issue.

Beryl has me in cotton wool and has forbidden me from ladders, stools, roofs, and anything higher than the sole of my socks. With me not being able to feature in any clean up duties it was left to my son Darryl. He sold off any thing that could be sold.

On a visit prior to my accident, I contacted the old woollen mill which is now a marketplace selling any and everything. It was arranged that they would advertise our wares to stall holders. Covid 19 had arrived as we were preparing for sale. Rules were established by Government that a clearance sale or sale of any type was forbidden. Enough people had seen the flyers that I had circulated and arranged with Darryl for private viewings. He sold lots of items in the next week or so. Along with the private sales there were plenty of tip visits, house cleaning, shed cleaning as well as him working in Melbourne some 130 Kms way.

    He had met a new lady, Lisa Foley, who became a great asset to him helping most weekends. Lisa's father and stepmother, Trevor and Barb Denham from Somerville was seconded by Darryl and Lisa to lend a helping hand. They were a great help with Trevor building the destroyed veranda roof. Slowly but surely, Darryl reached the end to this monstrous clean up.

RICKETSIA.

    Over 147 years rats, mice and rabbits lived in and around the sheds. Their droppings, urine and diseases were evidently present in bags, straw and junk. Unfortunately, Darryl become quite ill after he had moved out of the property. Doctors could not identify his illness until one doctor tested him for an animal to human disease and found he had contacted Rickettsia. This disease is not transferrable between humans. It is mainly found in the tropics and spread by a Tick. This has laid Darryl low for over 12 months. It saps energy, gives heart attack symptoms and causes constant sweating which effects sleeping and general well- being. Lisa is looking after him, God bless this lovely lady. Who knows how long it will take until he is cured and allow him to return to full employment?

Thank God for the insurance plan he has as this has given him a portion of his wage.

With the sale now well and truly completed, I have advanced the boys a bit of money in advance of my death. I thought it better to hear a thank you and feel a handshake before my demise.

TAXATION

I found out that all good things come to an end. The taxman wasn't real kind to me due to the taxation rules. I was obliged to pay CGT (Capital Gains Tax). The rules were such that I had never lived in the house or on the property, so CGT was applicable. The only problem to me was the amount. Beryl said to me, "With all the windfalls and eBay sales, you have the money so pay it and stop complaining". Sound advice.

Chapter 17

THE HADFIELD FOOTBALL CLUB BALL and the DISASTER.

All dressed up and ready to party.

As mentioned on page 50, I would give an update on the 50th anniversary if and when it took place.
On April 2nd, 2022, the Ball finally came to fruition and as promised I now write my update although it is a subject my wife Beryl and I would like to forget.

This time the Ball was not postponed. It was all stations go. We set off from Forster with our best finery, we were determined to impress and do ourselves proud. Beryl with her Green Gown and me with my dinner Suit and bowtie.

We arrived in Melbourne on the Friday prior, to stay a few days with Graeme and Norma, my brother and sister-in-law at Templestowe. They have a big and beautiful home and run a successful business in the food providing sector. I think Graeme was proud of his big brother's achievements, providing us with his firms hire-car and driver for the night at his expense. Nothing was left to chance on this night of nights, as we thought.

We arrived at the Hyatt in Essendon Fields at 6.45pm, a little early and very toey. Peter Whittle, our escort for the night was there waiting for us. All was starting to excite me. I had written out the questions they were to ask me, practicing my reply with the written answers forming my speech. I was not sure if the occasion was going to get to me. I'm afraid it got to me in spades for reasons we did not contemplate. Read on.

Yes, it was fortunate to write out the questions because by the time I was called up as first speaker I was a total mess after having an altercation with security over COVID and Beryl being refused entry and sent home leaving me there to battle nerves, extreme disappointment and anger. I entered the ball room, within 10 minutes of being told that Beryl would not be allowed entry and having a half hour interrogation with security. I was introduced to the numbers present, called to the stage and questioned on the formation of the club. (See Questions and Answers attached)

To be honest, I was not in the mood or the position to be called upon to do the job that I had dreamed of for months and travelled 1100 Kms for. I was in tears for my wife, choked with anger and disbelief. I was a mess. As they say in show business, THE SHOW MUST GO ON. I did my best, after a time I settled down to a point where I stopped the tears and choking on words. Somehow, I got through it and received great applause. During the night I got pats on the back and thanks for setting up the Hadfield Football Club all those fifty years ago.

I have taken the Hyatt to task as can be seen by the following letter. I am still in communication with their management. It is hoped I can give you the final wash up before publication of my story.

Questions prepared for me and my answers for the 50th year Anniversary of the Hadfield Football Club.

Q1. Who would have thought that after 51 years we would be celebrating Hadfield's half century?
A1. Probably not too many? I am sure some of the Foundation committee would have had a dream of its success at the very best. People such as Leon Coventry {1st secretary) John Walker (1st Treasure) Ron Waugh, Kevin Dempsey. and Alan Kennedy would have had a belief. Leon Coventry and myself were dead sure it would last.

- Q2. What drew yow to the area and what was your motivation to lead the club.
- A2. There is not a short answer to this question so bear with me.
    I had lived in Hadfield since 1959. It was a vastly different place back then.
    There was neither made roads or footpaths.
    no sewerage system. Pan once a week.

no telephone.

no football club.

in fact, no nothing.

I played for Moonee Valley from 1958, after having 2 years with Carlton 3rds. I coached the Valleys in 1965. They did not like my disciplinary rules, so I got the sack after one year.

Ascot Youth Centre (AYC) recruited me as playing coach in 1966. We won the premiership being undefeated grand champions. Eat your heart out Moonee Valley. I coached AYC again in 1967 to when they amalgamated with Riverside Stars in 1968, I retired.

Leon Coventry and Kevin Dempsey heard of my coaching ability and asked me to coach The Hadfield Youth Club Football Club coaches as they were high on enthusiasm but light on ability, I gave it a go and coached the under 15s as their coach suffered a work injury during 1969.

The following year. 1970, I was elected President of Hadfield Youth Club Football Club and coached the under 11s.

Leon and I after a footy meeting at Reddish reserve discussed, under a street light, a break away from the Youth Club mentality. We took our desire to the Youth Club committee. They eventually agreed and was to give us all their footy gear. We got 10 t0 12 moth eaten green and gold jumpers from their existing 4 teams, we accepted their "gift" and started the long road.

Leon said to me, "We will be in the VFA within 5 years". He was so confident of the long-term outcome.

In answer to the motivations part of your question.

My motivation was to lead the club in a professional way to give the kids of the area a real football club and for them to aspire to our brand-new open age team. This could not have been done or possible in a youth Club environment.

Q3   You were president for 3 years, talk us through those initial years because we are to mention, we won a senior premiership and an under 11s in our first year.

A3   Actually I was president for 7 years. One with the youth club and 6 with the Hadfield Football Club. Well, where do I start, they were tough years. Things we had to do so that we could start 1971, the new era, with 4 underage teams and our brand-new senior side.

      a. Find a league for our seniors.

We had two choices, the Northern District League and the Essendon District League. I was well known in the EDFL through Moonie valley and AYC, so we arranged a meeting with President McTaggart and Secretary Marcy of the EDFL, we were finally accepted into the C Grade division.

      b. Raise money, we had zero.

Buy jumpers for 5 teams,

Pay ground rental.

Pay affiliation fees.

Survive

      c. Write a constitution.

      d. Find suitable ground as the Hadfield High Schools was not suitable.

      e. Fix Reddish to make it useable.

      f. Find players for our open age side.

      g. Find an off the hook jumper. We choose Hawthorn's as their colours were not used in either the juniors or open age leagues. As well as the off the hook colours, we adapted their song and of course the Mighty Hawk.

All this whilst I was coaching the under 11s to the clubs FIRST Premiership

Some other things that happened were:

      a. A player's rebellion and strike.

      b. To show we meant business, the committee took the field with underage kids and got belted.

     b. A player given a life sentence for striking an umpire. This action and the fact we transported the umpire to hospital kept us in the EDFL.

     c. The formation of a Ladies Committee. They operated from a tent in the early stage There was a lot more, enough to give you ulcers.

     Due to the time constraint per speaker, a lot has to be left un-said.

Q4. Do I check the scores each week?

A4. I keep across whatever is on the web site. Sally McKercher has been keeping me up to date with Yes, the Ball is on, No, it's off. To finally, here we are tonight celebrating a milestone which was born 51 years ago under the streetlight outside the Reddish Reserve Pavilion.

Thank you to the club for the invitation to me and my wife Beryl. A crying shame that an incident by the security on entry has spoilt the occasion for us both. Sorry for my crippling speech. I am really wrecked.

Thank you for listening to my story as disjointed as it was.

We have travelled 1100 Kms each way for this celebration. I would not have missed it for the world. I worked bloody hard for the Hadfield Football Club and still love it to death. **GO THE HAWKS**

I have taken the Hyatt to task as can be seen by the following letter. I am still in communication with their management. It is hoped I can give you the final wash up before publication of my story.

My letter to Hyatt Management

General Manager
Hyatt Hotel
Essendon Fields.

I bring to your attention, the function held on Saturday 2nd April 2022 at your Hyatt Hotel Ballroom in Essendon Fields.

The function was the 50th year formation celebrations of The Hadfield Football Club.

I, Neville Fox (aged 83 plus) together with my wife Beryl (aged 85 plus) of 34 Daphne St Forster 2428 were VIP guests to this much awaited and prestigious night of nights.

At the formation of the Club in 1971 I was elected as inaugural and founding president, a position I held for six years. I was also awarded the Club's first Life Membership. I am so proud.

Due to heavy – handed and bully behaviour by your Security Superintendent Leon (surname I have forgotten) it turned out to be a monumental embarrassing and social standing destroyer to us both. It was supposed to be the much awaited, treasured nights of all nights to both myself and to The Hadfield Football Club. A celebration that I had worked so very hard and diligently for, all those 51 years ago.

A Summary of the Early Stages of the Destroyed Night.

Arrived per hire car from Templestowe at 6.45pm at Hotel Hyatt Essendon Fields.

Confronted at entrance by security staff demanding QR on entry.

Unable to oblige as we are from NSW and not having Vic credentials.

Requested Vaccination certificates. I obliged with mine as it was on my phone.

My wife could not as she was dressed in an elegant ball gown carrying a small accessory purse.

No room for her phone. This form of entry to functions has been phased out in NSW.

Discussion took place with your Security Man. After some minutes of explaining he allowed us entry.

During this time a multitude of guests had entered without QR coding or showing Vacs certificates.

We mingled with other guests until 7pm, door opening.

Just prior to entering the hall your Security Supervisor, Leon? (Forgotten his name, starts with L, I think), summoned us to a poorly lit conference room for his interrogation. This type of security sanctioning has been long gone in NSW. We had no fear of his interrogation.

Not being able to meet his order/demand to show credentials, he bullied and pressured my wife to do a RAT test or he would prevent her entry.

I was endeavouring to have her Vaccination certificate sent to my phone.

Keeping in mind we are 83 and 85 liaising with people of similar age. Not really tech savvy.

In due course I obtained the information demanded but was told by Security, "Too late I have commenced RAT testing. If you had of obtained it five (5) minutes earlier, you would be in the hall by now."

Of course, I argued, but no, your man was determined to make his mark and our night hell.

The RAT returned, in his estimation, a positive reading. A very weak pink line that was vaguely evident at the very best but not conclusive.

He had handled the RAT packaging and contents deciding a second RAT test was necessary.

The second RAT test showed a similar result to the first.

He would not listen to reason telling me there was a $300,000 fine if he "broke the law". I told him that I was prepared to pay the fine. "No" was his sharp reply.

I suggested a quarantine area in the back of the hall. Again, "No" was his arrogant reply.

It was explained to him that we both had RAT tests on Wednesday 30/3/22 to make sure we were good to go on Thursday 31/3/22. No symptoms prevailed. "Sorry", was his feeble response.to this information.

He was reminded again that a multitude had entered about 7pm without challenge, where damage, if any, could have started. He showed no interest, for some reason he wanted us to suffer.

At approximately 7.30pm, my wife with tears streaming down her face told me to enter the function as this was my night of nights and she would re-book the hire car and return to Templestowe. This was the only answer left to us. Your man showed a lack of people skills and workplace diplomacy.

I entered the function at 7.35pm and was called to the stage at 7.40pm to give my speech on the trials and tribulations of the formation of the Hadfield Football Club. This was the most difficult thing that I had been called on to do in my living memory.

Through choking words, unable to speak at times, tears of hurt and embarrassment, I managed to provide an uninspiring delivery to a subject that had meant so much to me for 51 years.

After it being postponed four times then having to put up with your supervisor who is severely lacking in people skills and workplace diplomacy I was shattered.

I salute the Hadfield organizing committee for standing by me throughout this torturous encounter.

I also make mention of our hire car driver who spoke to your supervisor when picking up my wife, he was told by your supervisor "I don't believe she has ever had vaccinations." He is prepared to be witness to that remark.

She also tested NEGATIVE to RAT tests on Sunday 3/4/22 at 10am and on Monday 4/4/22 when we visited my sister at the Warramunda Nursing Home KYABRAM.

In conclusion to this, most soul destroying, embarrassing, humiliating and torturous night I am forced to request some recompense from your Hotel Hyatt to cover my costs etc.

Petrol for 2485 Kms return	$ 341.35
Motels. 2 @ $130 per night	$ 260.00
Function tickets 2 @ $190 each	$ 380.00
Incidentals Dinner Suit hire and food	$ 350.00
Hire car 3 trips @$100 per trip	$ 300.00
Total	**$1635.00**

I sincerely hope that this unfortunate incident can be settled without having to take it further.

Again, I emphasise "This night of nights can never, never be re-visited".

I await you and your management's reply.

yours Truly
Neville Fox

    Nothing was heard back from The Hyatt leaving me thinking I had lost the fight.
On Thursday April 22nd, 3 weeks after the event I received a phone call from the General Manager apologizing for not attending to the matter earlier. He had been on leave in Queensland.
He was devastated with his Security Officer. For twenty minutes we talked and listened, his voice was full of remorse, anguish, and emotion. He has asked me not to take the matter further promising to get back to me with some form of recompense.
    I await his further contact with me but if it was only words and no action, I will be making more of it.
    The General Manager has been in touch with me promising to give recompense. In the meanwhile, he sent flowers to Beryl for her Mother's Day. Advised me that he has demoted his supervisor for insensitive behaviour and to have more training in public relations. I wait for further dialogue.

Further contact was made on Friday 13/5/22.

    Latest and possibly the end to our torturous trip.
I have been offered $950 as recompense which covers a good percentage of my out-of-pocket expenses. I have asked for him to up the sum but doubt if that will happen. I suppose the result is better than nothing.

CHAPTER 18

CONCLUSION

I have never written anything like this. I am not an author. I don't profess to be anything but an 84-year-old man with a desire to tell my story my way, with WARTS and ALL.
There is lots more I could add to my story, I have picked out things that are informative to my family, hoping these will not be lost over time.
I have included some humorous topics in the hope of not boring my readers. All in all it has been interesting to tackle a life story.

We, Beryl, and I, are very happy in the life we now live. I just hope our lives continue with good health, good friends, 3 good meals a day and half a bed. Times have been good to us for our thirty plus years together. Naturally we have had illnesses along the way together with my accidents but that is part and parcel of life. Hopefully there is at least another ten years that awaits us.

It is my hope that my children and their children together with the descendants of the Fox family keep one of these books so that they know something of the hard ships, disappointments, conquests, and achievements obtained by those before them.

Some thing to be proud of. Through out my life In sport and Clubmanship I have gained recognition of the highest standards. You can't obtain three life memberships from vastly different persuasions unless you give your all. I believe I have done that to every thing throughout my eighty four years. A lesson for any one that cares to read my story is to put in and help no matter what the case. Whether it be work, sport, volunteering, family, or just being nice to your fellow man. JUST PUT IN.

Some more pictures of Forster

Water craft entertaining swimmers in the "Rock Pool" Tuncurry

The bridge in the distant background linking Forster on the left and Tuncurry on the right.

The bridge is 631 meters long and 13.5 meters wide. It was officially opened on July 18 1959.

Forster's maine beach and sea baths known as The Bull Ring.

The old Club house on the way to demolishment. Now a car park.

The Tuncurry Golf Club's New Clubhouse.   Drinks after the game.

Forster Club House. Headquarters of Forster Tuncurry Golf Club.

Forster's 2nd Fairway and Green.

Rear of Forster Club House over loking course.

Practice Putting Green

The 631-metre bridge linking Forster and Tuncurry.

Machinery you would find on the farm.

Wagon used for carting in Hay

Hay-rake for cocking hay

Gig/Sulky going to town.

Plough for Cultivating paddocks.

Fergie Tractor.

Chapter 19

ADDENDUM and POSTSCRIPTS

. My sons loan. Page 125

.The Lift. Page, 125 to 126

.The trip to talk about for ever. Pges 126 to 131

. Graeme's farewell to his business life and Doris's farewell to life. Pages 131, 133

A few stories that maybe handy and informative to future readers.

Both my sons, Greg and Darryl, have put their loan monies to good use. They have both purchased a home each in Townsville QLD. I have called the advancements a loan so that it can be called in if I so desire. Both have agreed in writing to my conditions.

Greg has good reason to pick that part of the world, he has a son Brendan and a daughter Nikki and their children living there. There is a good chance his other daughter, Elysha, will shift in the near future.

Darryl has very recently purchased there. This has been a dream of his for some time. It makes a nice little family of my two sons and Greg's off spring's. Darryl has waited for about twelve months to make the move. Unfortunately, he and Lisa have parted company after much procrastinating re the shift north. It appears that he has everything in order with his children who will stay in Moama and holiday in Townsville. He has the understanding and agreement of their mother.

I believe both have purchased well. I await positives for a bright and better future for both.

LIFT 11/ 7/22 our lift was installed and commissioned by CMC Lifts. Now we are ready to take on older age. Darren's tradies did a top job. If you ever want a lift provided and installed, CMC Lifts are the ones to talk to.

The following is unbelievable. No sooner the lift, ensuite and "old age rails" were installed, Beryl fell and broke her hip. This happened when she was at a funeral on the 20/9/22 and I was installing the last railing, see picture.

Surely, someone must have been watching every move. There can be no other explanation. In the space of two months the lift was a necessity. Unbelievable.

The last safety rails.

THE TRIP TO TALK ABOUT FOREVER

I could not let this book go to final print without this story being included. It is probably in the wrong order but to my way of thinking it's a story that happened very recently and deserves the final place of my life's memories.

I always wanted to visit and fly the Kimberley and Bungle Bungles, at last it is about to happen. A coach trip leaving Forster on 1st August 2022 at 7am picking up passengers along the way to Taree where we did an about turn and headed back to Nabiac then to Gloucester via Thunderbolts Way for our lunch stop at Walcha. Following lunch, it was all aboard for our first overnight stop at Moree. We travelled 623 Kms enjoying the scenic different countryside through wind, rain, and cloud. After a good rest at the Burke and Wills followed by a hearty breakfast, we hit the road at 8.30 am for our second day with two extra passengers from Peterborough. They flew from Peterborough to Moree, like others further along the way not wanting to miss the trip. Steve Gatland, the tour organiser, and sole driver  purchased Subway sandwiches and rolls for our lunch at St George on the banks of the Balonne River. Prior to lunch we stopped at Thallon to view the silo paintings. In the PM we progressed to Tambo via Augathella and Moven. A very long day of 750 Kms arriving at 6.45 pm. Long days, to me are expected in the early stages on a trip of this calibre, a trip of over 5000 Kms in 14 days, catering for the needs and accommodation of 45 passengers. Also, the places of interest had to be addressed in the operators planning. A big job.

  After being well fed and watered we departed for The Stockman's Hall of Fame and/or The Qantas Air Museum for a 2 hour stop at Longreach. For the first time we had to buy own lunch. Back on the coach and off to the Dinosaur Museum a very interesting afternoon being lectured on these millions of year-old creatures in the exhibition centre

prior to visiting their workshops where bones are separated and collated. This Dinosaur display is much better than the Footprint display centre further out of

Winton which I visited some years ago. After a busy day we arrived in Winton to enjoy dinner at Tattersalls Hotel to await the Waltzing Matilda exhibition first thing on day 4. Day 3 was a shorter drive day covering 521 Kms.

Winton is a very clean, vibrant country town heavily dependent on tourism. The main street is wide with lovely old buildings, alfresco dining, an outdoor picture theatre, Arno's famous wall of every and anything jammed in concrete forming a wall of about 50 meters long. (A must see) The Dinosaurs, Waltzing Matilda, which is unbelievable since it's rebuilt, numerous caravan parks and motels. Winton should be a must on your visit list. Leaving at 10.30 am for our lunch stop at the McKinlay Hotel for a sandwich lunch, supplied. The famous Blue Healer pub was by passed on route to the more famous McKinlay pub. It is known worldwide as The Crocodile Dundee Walkabout Hotel featuring in the Paul Hogan film Crocodile Dundee. From McKinlay we headed for Mt Isa for day 5s camp Our distance for day 5 was

Me with Crocodile Dundee

670Kms, the second most for the entire venture. A swim in the pool, dinner, and day 6s breakfast it was then off to Tennant Creek at 9.30 am. On route, a comfort stop at Camooweal made famous by Slim Duty's, Ballad of Camooweal. Over the Northern Territory boarder with a time adjustment, for lunch at Barkley Homestead then further on to Tennant Creek. Steve our driver took on fuel and committed the biggest day light robbery in Tennant Creek's history. He filled his tanks to the brim with diesel, jumped into the driver's seat and drove out to our motel. It suddenly dawned on him that he had not paid. A phone call to the service station with a promise to return and pay prevented Steve being charged with the biggest day light robbery in Tennant Creek's history.

Day 6 of our tour was a low distance day of 410 Kms. Leaving Tennant Creek at 9 am, we progressed northward for a comfort stop at Renner Springs before arriving at Newcastle Waters Ghost Town for provided lunch. We explored the remains of the 1960 buildings of the pioneering days of drovers and their families. A public school still operates. Jones's store and the Junction Hotel are preserved along with historical landmarks of a lone stockman situated in the Drovers Memorial Park. A must see. The Ghost Town was the junction of three main overland stock routes where stores and provisions were obtained by the drovers. A lake adjacent to the road attracts great numbers of water birds after rains. After exploring the numerous relics, we make tracks to the Historic Pub of Daly Waters where comfortable accommodation awaits us along with an experience to remember for ever. The pub is of corrugated iron draped with bougainvillea's and crammed with decades of memorabilia. Evidently the girls leave bra, nickers and dress items of all colours, sizes, and style to hang proudly throughout the pub. There are more number plates, old currency, thongs, and quaint signage on display. Opposite the pub is Jim's Junk Yard displaying many restored cars, buses, motor bikes and more memorabilia. A dinner in their outside lounge area followed by a country and western singer who encouraged much dancing until stumps at 9.30 made for a truly fabulous night.

The pub dates back to 1934 serving passengers on Qantas using the first international runway in Australia. The pub has held a continuous licence since 1938. On the day we were there a Rodeo was held at the sports ground swelling the hundreds enjoying the atmosphere that this place generates with its quaintness. **A MUST STAY AND SEE**.

Reflections

Day 7, after another hearty breakfast it was push on to Katherine for lunch where two more joined us from Chinchilla Qld. After lunch a trip down "Nitmilik Gorge" travelling through two gorges for about 12 Kms passing under 70-meter-high cliffs. Very picturesque with enlightening talks by the guides showing how the big rains devour the gorges to a vastly different viewing from one season to the next.

We retired to the Pine Tree Motel where a swim was had by a few prior to a pool side dinner and drinks were served topping off another enjoyable day. Our shortest day's distance of 230 Kms.

Day 8 Katherine NT to Kununurra WA where we gained 90 minutes. Morning tea provided, was at Victoria River Roadhouse under shady trees whilst staring at the wonders of the outback. This country is vast and awe-inspiring. Victoria River Crossing is 194 Km s west of Katherine. Stopping at Timber Creek Roadhouse for a provided lunch then onto Argyle Homestead Museum. This part of our journey features an abundance of BOAB trees. We took time out to visit Kelly's Knob taking photos of Ord River Irrigation area and Mirima National Park. Eventually we arrive for day 8 and day 9 stays at the Kununurra Hotel. Kununurra is a relatively young booming town of 61 years old, situated on the eastern edge of the Kimberley. Today's travel was 520 Kms of hard but beautiful countryside. The rugged countryside changes every few kilometres. I could not suffer with boredom in the outback. The word Kununurra means Goonoonoorrang which means big water and big water is seen in all directions with the Ord River feeding into the man-made freshwater Lake Argyle. This expanse of water made by the dam wall makes the Sydney harbour look like a pond. It holds 10.7 billion cubic meters of water 18 times that of the Sydney Harbour and is known as the freshwater sea. On the morning of day 9 we rise very early to board a flight at 5.15 am over the Bungle Bungles. This was the day I have been waiting for. I was not disappointed. Beneath the plane rich agriculture farms are seen. Cotton, crop, fruit, vegetables can be seen. This is the result of the abundance of water. Also, to be witnessed was the beehive like striped domed rock formations. All in all, this was a wonderful 2-hour experience. A packed breakfast hamper was supplied, and we were then off for a Lake Argyle and Ord River discovery cruise. A swim with BBQ provided lunch and drinks together with our guide captain Guy who was entertaining and informative while looking out for fresh water crocodiles, bird life, rock wallabies and more.

Following our morning cruise, it was back on the Triple J Tour bus to drive across the Ord Top Dam wall with a view of the Hydro Power Station before boarding the Triple J boat for a 55 Km Ord River journey back to Kununurra marvelling at the spectacular scenery, wildlife, flora and fauna along the way including the fresh water crocodiles. An afternoon tea in a hide away river side camp was one out of the blue. We were treated with a colourful sunset and reflections before re-boarding our bus and returning to our accommodation where our dinner was served closing out an amazing day.

Day 10. Depart Kununurra hotel at 9 am for a visit to the Sandalwood shop where we had the opportunity to learn about the Sandalwood processing journey and experience the extensive range of skin care products manufactured in their Albany distillery. The ladies on our trip appeared to love the fragrance of soaps and lotions. At 11 am we arrive at the Kimberley Ornamental Stone Shop. It was amazing what the craftsmen can make out of the Zebra Rock and other Siltstones unique to the East Kimberley. After a lunch provided it was off on a 4-hour trek to Halls Creek some 360 Kms south where gold was first discovered. In 1885 a 28-ounce nugget was found by Charles Hall.

Unfortunately for me this is where my much-awaited WA trip came to an early end. Arriving at the Kimberley Hotel we did the same as we had done every day, unload our luggage, get our room number and key then proceed to our deluxe room. I had to pull my case up a steep path when a gunshot sounded in my left calf muscle followed by the unravelling of my muscle fibres, like a spring unravelling. I had torn the muscle and was immediately in excruciating pain. I hobbled with aid to the bar area to get ice to stem the internal bleeding. A nurse with good intent suggested she take me to the hospital for treatment and hopefully be able to continue. On entering the hospital their first job was to test for COVID. The result was a positive read which meant I and Beryl were quarantined for 7 days and off the last section of the trip. Once positive you are under the WA government and health department. I was ordered into a hospital house for the next 7 days, as I thought. But no, next morning two nurses checked me out and said that a room was available at the hotel, and we were to accept it. We were punted back to the hotel but not to the lovely deluxe room but to a dingy 5 x 4 metre dog box at $230 per day plus food. We had a bathroom, a kitchenette with no light. There was one light only with a very dim globe. There was a TV but no instructions and no station guide. I learnt how to drive it, fortunately it had FOXTEL which helped pass the time. There is no internet, no Optus mobile service. Any messages had to be sent to the hotel and hand delivered to our room, number 30. The hospital was able to get us on to Telstra where we again could communicate with the outside world. The Management was told of the short falls but said to us "what is, is. Beryl was allowed out to shop for some food to minimize costs. Even though we have insurance we did not know what would be covered, we took the safety-first tact supplying ourselves with breakfast and lunches.

As I write this, we have arranged a bus to Broome leaving at 5.45 am on 18/8 via Fitzroy Crossing, one night's accommodation in Broome and a flight to Newcastle via Melbourne departing at 11.40 am on Friday 19/8/22. As our luck held true to form, the Newcastle leg was running late. We touched down at 9.55 just avoiding the Newcastle 10 pm curfew. Beryl's brother Ron, was there to transport us to Forster arriving at 12.05 am. The trip is over THANK GOODNESS we are home at last.

Going back to Wednesday 17th, a once in a lifetime experience occurred. We decided to leave our dog box a little early and have a much-deserved drink at the swimming pool bar. A group of 24 motor home travellers walked through the bar area. One of them stopped, stood, and stared at me. He said to me, "Is your name Steele" My reply was a firm "No" His next words were, "If you are not Steele, you must be Fox" I sat there dumb founded with mouth wide open thinking, "who the hell is this bloke" Finally, he removed his cap and said, "I'm Dolly, (Allan Dalton) Hadfield's coach of the 1989 premiership side and second speaker behind you at Hadfield's 50th year anniversary ball". (See reference on pages 112—119). Fancy bumping into someone I had not seen or spoken to in many years and meeting him in the God Forsaken town of Halls

Creek about 5000 Kms from nowhere. I apologized for my effort in delivering my speech at the ball due to the banning of Beryl into the ballroom. He said, "Under the circumstances you were terrific. You should have Hadfield archive and post it in a prominent place as you gave me and everyone in attendance an insight into how this wonderful club started and is still going strong. If your information is not archived and/or published, the true Hadfield will never be known. You are the last connection. Now think about it".

After getting his inspiring spiel, I have requested the Hadfield Committee do as he suggested. I await their response.

Through our forced stay, we met some lovely people, Grace cleaner and bar supervisor, Troy the office manager, Mick the welder and maintenance man. He was a rough, untidy larrikin of about 60 years with a heart of gold. Peta the manager was no way near the rank-and-file workers. She could/would not help us to the 5.45 am bus to Broome. This place does not have cabs. Beryl rang the hospital; they were only too happy to help us. At 5 am Mick knocked on our door stating that Peta had offered him her car to get us to the bus. Her conscious may have got the better of her. Mick was not required as the hospital had everything covered. Mick told me that he started early using her car to check the security, eating up time while being paid overtime. A win for Mick.

The 9-hour, 690 Km trip to Broome via Fitzroy Crossing was for ever changing with scenery of farmland, desert, and everything in between. Boab trees (Adansonia gregorii in the Melvaceae family) were abundant as they are native to northern West Australia and Northern Territory.

We met an interesting artist on board who gave Beryl one of his hand painted rocks. We bunkered down in the Broome Time Resort, a lovely motel then off to see the sunset, have dinner and a few drinks at Cable Beach.

Next morning, Friday 19th August we bid WA farewell as we caught the plane to the Eastern states and finally to 34 Daphne St Forster which we call home arriving at midnight. The others on the trip left Broome on 14th August 2022 at 11.25 am arriving in Sydney 10.15 pm via Brisbane staying overnight then coach to Forster included in package.

In summing up the trip, I would advise it to be a must for people interested in our vast, awe-inspiring, picturesque, and wonderful landscape with an abundance of different fauna and flora. The majority of the 5300 kms is unbelievable. **GO SEE IT FOR YOURSELF.**

Graeme's Farewell to his business and Doris's Farewell to Life..

An invitation to my brother Graeme's party for the sale of his excellent business was nothing less than first class. He started off in the dye industry and progressed into food additives and pill colouring supplying the world with his products. The party was held on December 11th, 2022, at the Park Hyatt Melbourne, an extravaganza not to be missed. We were wined and dined on the best of everything. My estimated cost of $30k would by near the mark. He could well afford the estimated sum as he got many millions for his business and deserved every cent.

The sad thing was the absence of our sister Doris. (Dorrie to me) She was in the Shepparton hospital with a broken hip. Fortunately, we were able to see her on 13th December whilst in Victoria. She was in a very bad way and her days were numbered. Dorie was returned to her own bed in the Warramunda Nursing Home on 21st December and passed away on 26th December. She was remarkable a day or two before her death, she sat up in bed, had her hair done and reading Christmas cards. It was her final "light before the storm.". She looked at peace.

Her death prompted another trip to Kyabram to attend her funeral. I gave a small eulogy to the 100 people in attendance at her grave side ceremony.

My short eulogy explaining my sister Dorrie, could have been reduced to two words. **Terrific sister.**

Dorie was a good sister. She was older and looked after me when I was becoming single. She would mend my clothes. Make sure I was eating properly. She was like a mum to me.

She was stubborn. Single minded, a real Fox taking after our father Harry. She was a very good mum and loving nana to all in her family.

To me and Beryl she was a dear friend, our first stop from NSW was the Vick household in Kyabram.

We would always find her at the sink preparing a meal.

After a meal was the problem, packing up dishes was always loud as she threw things left right and centre never breaking any, but the noise was unbelievable. There was always a friendly tease.

To brother Graeme and his wife Norma she was a solid loving friend, sister and in- law.

In fact, she loved them along with Beryl and me.

In saying that, Dorrie had a great life of caring for those she loved. She will be sadly missed, there will be no more of the DO YOU REMEMBER WHEN episodes. From here on it will be REMEMBER DORRIE.

God bless sister, REST IN PEACE DORRIE.

We spent a couple of days with Graeme and Norma prior to our return trip to Forster. The immediate Fox family is now reduced to two, Graeme at 82 and me at 84. We are both reasonably fit and hoping for another dozen years.

THE END

Hope you enjoyed my effort of telling my story my way.

www.ingramcontent.com/pod-product-compliance
Lightning Source LLC
Chambersburg PA
CBHW041712290426
44109CB00028B/2852